The Divine Order

Rediscover the
to restore you
and release y

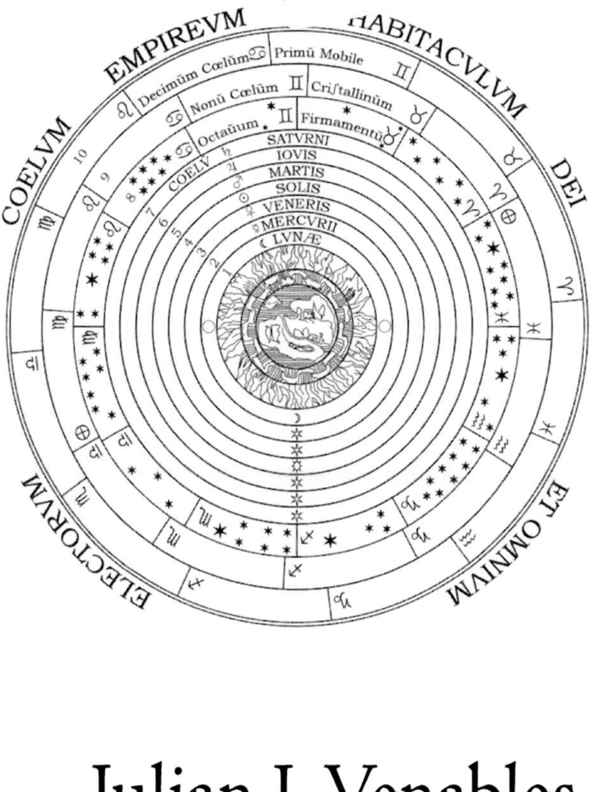

Julian J. Venables

ISBN 978-1-7392890-0-3

Layout and typography by Perceptia

Printed in Great Britain

Acknowledgements

The author has endeavoured to trace all copyright holders of images and/or other media included in this book. If anything has inadvertently been omitted, please contact us and we will make the necessary arrangements.

Image credits (Unsplash): andrew-spencer p. 49; ayo-ogunseinde p. 68; edi-libedinsky p. 73; giulia-may p. 48; jasper-wilde p. 67; jon-butterworth p. 21, p. 52; jongsun-lee p. 15; julia-kadel p. 44; karina-carvalho p. 67; khamkeo-vilaysing p. 14; todd-rhines p. 27; tolga-ahmetler p. 72

Disclaimer

The content and information contained in this book and its related website(s) is intended to be educational. It is provided in good faith but should not and cannot be a substitute for professional diagnostic or prescriptive medical, mental health, or spiritual counselling or treatment. The author strongly recommends anyone needing such help to obtain the appropriate professional help. No liability is accepted by the book's author and publishers for any physical, mental, emotional, problems caused as a result directly or indirectly from this book. The intent of the author is only to offer information of a general nature to help you in your quest for emotional and spiritual well-being. The author and the publisher are in no way liable for any misuse of the material and assume no responsibility for your actions.

Contents

1: Introduction

The Moon—Expressing feelings

☽

We each have our own path through life, but it is not always smooth. This book offers guidance, understanding, and happiness via something so simple that it is all around us, just needing to be unveiled.

Throughout your journey, have you had a nagging feeling that you haven't quite found it yet; there's something missing? Are you still asking "*What is the truth?*"

Modern western culture pushes us into the world, teaching us to direct our attention outwards. While it is important to face the world, perhaps the balance is not quite right. What if, like the ancients, we could learn to re-orientate ourselves to explore our inner world?

What if you could find your innermost centre and discover it is beautiful, enlightening, and divine? And this could allow you to refocus outwards to enjoy a whole new experience of life?

This book is a space-time map for self-improvement and personal development. It is written to help you become a more integrated, happier, and healthier person.

About this book

As the world faces ecological decimation, climate crisis, and social upheaval, there is an urgency to rediscover a new understanding of ourselves in the context of nature, ecosystems, and the environment. This promises not just practical and emotional benefits, but spiritual ones too; we can begin to understand better the development of the soul, appreciate and enjoy art, and by coming from a wellspring at the centre of our being, we can move into the light of divine truth.

This first book in a projected series starts with the author's personal journey (Part 2), introducing many important influences and explaining why this book became necessary to write. It is hoped that much of this story will resonate with the reader's own experience.

Part 3 gets into the nitty-gritty with a fact-filled overview of the planets, wherein the secrets reside. We learn about both the physical and metaphysical attributes of each planet, and also how they define and influence different archetypes within each of us.

Part 4 is pivotal and explains the full import of the subject of the title of this book, *The Divine Order*—in detail, it provides a historical background, a theoretical overview, and an analysis of how it fits into the typical lifeplan of all of us, offering some fascinating insights and revelations. These are powerful secrets indeed!

With the theory behind us, Part 5 turns to the highly practical, with a set of experiments intended to help with the process of refocussing to gain the full benefits of the knowledge gained so far. The activities are simple and easy to perform but profound in impact!

At this point, it becomes necessary to chart a path back from the revelations within to the outside world of everyday reality, and Part 6 does just that in a highly practical way, using the mechanism of a series of daily writing activities and guided meditations that can be performed over and over again.

Part 7 brings us firmly back to Earth again, with more practical examples and explanations of how to incorporate *The Divine Order* in everyday life.

Although this book is written for the nonspecialist, it covers some sophisticated concepts and a little specialised vocabulary is sometimes necessary. To this end, a glossary has been provided on page 125, and any words you find underlined like this can be checked there. We hope this is helpful!

Two further Addenda provide a brief introduction to the planetary hours (because hours also figure large as well as days in the grand scheme of things) introducing a unique and revolutionary method for finding them very simply without any maths; and an overview of planetary flow.

The Divine Order is an exciting revelation, and I'm sure you will love what you are about to discover. Above all, the book will allow you to change your viewpoint and perception of the universe around you. Once you experience this change, you can understand how the ancients saw the world and were able to connect to their divinity within as a part of creation.

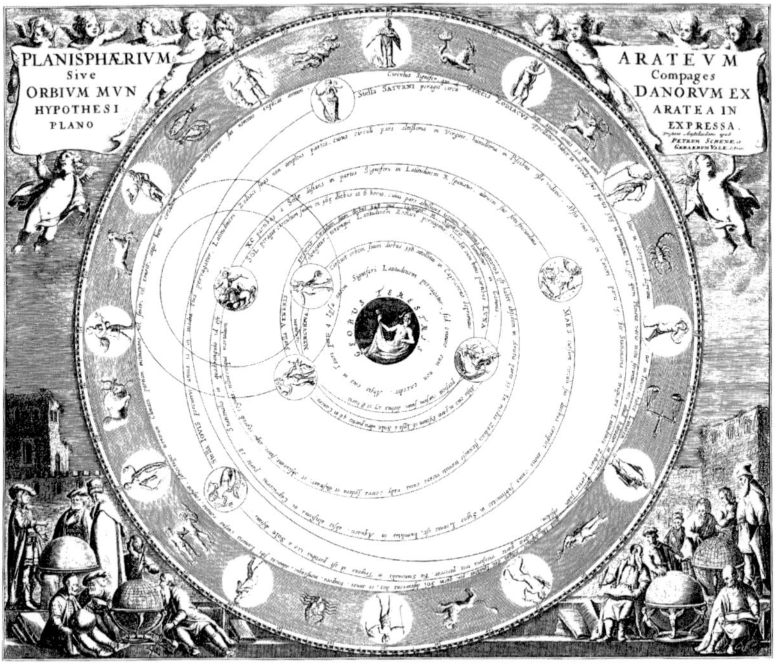

This understanding in itself will lead to greater internal peace, as you become more able to fathom the natural tides of the cosmos, reacting to them positively and drawing energy rather than resisting and denying the flow of consciousness.

This has the potential to supply all our requirements, including the need for self-validation through expression and creativity—engaging with the universe outside via the imagination inside us. When we use our imagination, we are not just making up things that are not there.

Imagination can clothe everything with meaning; it exists to make a synthesis of all we experience. The power of the imagination—conjured up in the mind's eye—can lead our conscious intentions, overriding decision-making faculties, attitudes, and methods of judgment without our even being aware of it. The methods this book reveals will demonstrate this, working through it, such that by becoming more conscious of what the mind's eye presents, we gain a more unified and cohesive picture of what we would like in our lives. It is about working with one's personal truth.

Although this book is complete within itself, the ideas is contains are so powerful that it will take a series to fully explore. Book 1—that you are reading now—is but the first part, laying down the theory while adding a complete *modus operandi* for dealing with modern life in a hugely practical way. As we mentioned earlier, it is clear that our own planet, the Earth, faces potential ecological disaster in the near future, and *The Divine Order*

has much to say on this topic. A holistic expansion of the theory to cover life on and of this planet will be the subject of a companion volume.

On the other hand, the planets are but a local—if powerful—force acting upon each of us, and there are other important artefacts out there beyond that impact on us with their various cycles, moving *The Divine Order* upwards and outwards into the wider universe surrounding us.

So now, it is finally time to fasten your seatbelt and prepare for the journey of a lifetime as we take you back to the dawn of human civilisation and forward to the present and future, across all of space, as we discover the lost secrets of the planets, restore our rightful place in the universe, and regain our creative genius via *The Divine Order*.

2: The Journey Begins

Mercury—Crossing the threshold

☿

I've always been on a search for the truth. A large part of my life has been a quest to seek out the meaning of that part of our existence that we can't necessarily see in the material world but perceive in our minds as a vast interior imaginative space. I came to realise that this space is linked to faith and beliefs; behind everything else, there appears to be—and surely *must* be—a higher intelligence.

I attempted to find this through theology, with the goal of finding divinity or enlightenment. All the religions pointed to a similar thing—eternal awareness at the centre of being, with a core of emptiness or the no-thing at centre. The experience of life—the soul's journey—was almost tangibly encased around this eternal awareness, within which lies the feeling and experience of divinity and a connection to the creator. By learning to become one with the creator (of whatever religion), then, enlightenment could be realised.

However, finding religions a little constricting for my liking, I accepted what I could from them and concluded that the practice and experience of unconditional love and compassion was at their base. Love springs forth from emptiness and the no-thing.

Looking further afield turned up astrology—the study of planetary movements. Here were the higher intelligences, the creative spirits that form our imaginations and realisation of consciousness. When I discovered astrology and completed my Diploma in the subject, I realised this was, in fact, spiritual intelligence. Astrology offered a self-knowing guide to full participation in life.

After twenty years as an astrologer, the loss of my father in 2015 clarified my emotional conflicts with a shock-filled awakening. I cried only once. On the day of his death, I saw his fingertips start turning blue about an hour after his final moments. That process of colour change began a metamorphosis within me too; for the first time, I was able to see, feel, and act in my own way.

A week later, at his funeral, I didn't feel much real grief. I watched as others sobbed and their emotions flowed. In the couple of years that followed, I went firstly through a chrysalis phase of self-doubt, but it slowly dawned on me that I could now recapture my original spark, never seen or acknowledged before. No longer would I expect criticism.

I remembered a period in my past, aged eleven, when my father had agreed with the school headmaster that I would drop down a year—my contemporaries would move up to the next class, I would stay at the same desk in the old class for another year, and younger pupils would rise from the year below. This was total emotional devastation. The humiliation, failure, and rejection struck a deep chord. There was nobody to turn to. I was rejected on all sides.

A limiting belief developed as an unconscious pattern making me play out the rejection again and again as I grew into adulthood. This difficult core belief was like an unconscious script, stuck in a loop.

I felt I wasn't the only one; maybe everybody in one way or another played out their repeating loops, their unconscious patterns or limiting beliefs, and there was a story behind each of those difficult patterns, a story that could be contained in different phases of life and personal development. And someone needed to tell that story out loud. I realised then how the limitless capacities of the human soul had been largely silenced by the modern world—even rejected, and this was possibly the root not only to my own issues but to those of others around me, and maybe even of the whole human race. As I searched for that story, I encountered many influences who have informed the writing of this book.

Plato

One notable example was Plato, who described the formation of creation and its impressive order and beauty. He believed it to be *spherical* because that shape is the most complete and perfect, and drew a parallel between the perfection of the sphere and the perfection of the form of the living creature, the model on which his cosmos is based. As we shall see later, this simplicity and perfection encompassed by the sphere was very influential in my development of the topic of this book.

William Shakespeare

Another important influence—and perhaps the world's greatest storyteller—is of course William Shakespeare. How was it possible that he could capture the whole of the human experience in his works, despite having such limited knowledge of the world, I wondered? A little investigation showed that Shakespeare most likely received the classical education known as the *trivium*, the three ways of logic, grammar, and rhetoric; and the *quadrivium*, the four ways of arithmetic, music, geometry, and astronomy; each was linked to a planet, and even today, at the Globe theatre in London, one can see the planets depicted as characters painted on the backdrops behind the orchestra. I started to realise that our ancestors knew a lot more than we are taught in school, including that the planets were more than just lumps of rock and gas but could be given a character, an *archetype*! Shakespeare's enlightened *all-round* education formed a solid foundation from which he could unleash his inner creativity but I realised then that everyone can harness that same inner creativity; it lies within just waiting to be released and must be part of the answer.

The Globe Theatre

Later on, I encountered Dante, whose 13th century poem *The Divine Comedy* describes the spiritual journey of the soul. In some ways, this mirrored his—and my own—experiences. Facing charges of corruption and nonpayment of fines, Dante was exiled from Florence, his hometown, losing his path and experiencing all the vices of human nature. In my own way, I too had spent some time lost, wandering through what felt like a wasteland of life and job possibilities, feeling that nothing was right for me. At the same time, contemporaries and friends were starting to settle down, finding jobs, building careers, and gaining security.

Dante

I ended up travelling the world, searching out and trying various enlightenment techniques, before finally coming across the one that brought me home, outlined below. Dante likewise gradually returned to living a virtuous life, and showed that there is always hope. One key facet of his writings which had a big impact, especially *The Inferno* and *The Paradise,* is the observation of a hierarchical aspect to nature; it is vital to find our place within a seemingly random and chaotic world, and having a clear vision of the underlying structure of the world around us is another important clue.

Each of these writers was like a piece of the puzzle in my own life; reading their metaphor and allegory answered my questions. The great mystery of why I felt so hurt at rejection and could not seem to fit in with the way of the world were starting to be answered.

Owen Barfield

However, the true beginning of my healing journey and the foundation of this book was through the discovery of mindfulness and meditation. When looking at the inward aspects of our life experience, I started to recognise the mystical level where we can embody infinite space and "discover the inside of the whole world," as theorised by philosopher Owen Barfield (friend of C. S. Lewis and member of the Inklings group at Oxford university, along with J. R. R. Tolkien).

And so we arrive at the present. My search for meaning led to my becoming a professional astrologer. I realised I was searching for the real me, because of deep wounds somewhere in my unconscious. Reflecting on the past was painful, sometimes even stalling progress completely. I had an embedded unconscious pattern that had the power to keep me dissociated, vague, and unmotivated. Often I was lost before I had even started. Working through all these traumas and issues, as well as travelling the world and experiencing many things and meeting a huge variety of people—many of whom had issues similar to mine—encouraged me to assimilate everything into a new way of looking at the world, to find solutions, both for me and for others.

The solution needs to be built on the truth; especially the metaphysical wisdom of the ancients who were able to see things more clearly and without the distractions of modern life. It needs to be guided by solid theoretical foundations, with plenty of examples to illuminate and illustrate it, and have practical and creative applications to restore our rightful place in the universe. This solution is found within the truth of *The Divine Order,* and having spent many years refining and using this knowledge, it is now time to share it, which is the aim of this book. Let's start by taking a look at the planets.

3: The Lost Secrets

Venus—Discovering relationships within the cosmos

♀

Let us go back to the dawn of human civilisation. Imagine a time with no technology—no Internet, mobile phones, cars, or even electric power. So, there are no street lamps creating light pollution, and the night sky is filled with stars. The ancients, over generations, start to notice that while millions of these pinpoints of light appear fixed in a **firm**ament, just seven seem to move freely, as if of their own freewill. These are named "wanderers" or "planets" (*planētēs* in Greek) and are seen as gods or living creatures. Over the centuries, they receive names and characters. This section provides an overview of these planets. The order we are going to take is as follows:

The Moon
Mercury
Venus
The Sun
Mars
Jupiter
Saturn

Now, at this early stage, you may be questioning many things. Where's the Earth in the list? Surely the Sun is a *star* not a *planet* and should come first—even a *child* knows that!

For now, we humbly request our reader to go along with this order, with a degree of suspension of disbelief and trust, and all will be revealed. Suffice to say, for our purposes, the Moon and Sun are treated as planets, and we will be following the order on page 13.

To understand the lost secrets, we must refer to wisdom and connections intensely familiar to the ancients but since ignored and gradually lost over the centuries, a process hastened by the scientific revolution. We now take you on a guided tour of these seven relevant planets, showing how they appear in the sky and how each governs very specific aspects of our world.

The seven planets

We will examine the seven heavenly bodies in turn, looking at both their physical aspects and also beneath the surface to their more metaphysical qualities and interpretations.

☽ The Moon

We begin with the Moon, our constant companion who lights the night sky. Here are some basic facts to present a picture of the Moon as a physical object in the sky above us—the Moon of the astronomers. How many of these do you know? Do you find any of them surprising?

Fact File: The Moon In the sky

Size: One-quarter the size of the Earth; 2,160 miles in diameter

Distance: 239,000 miles from the Earth

Chemical Composition: crust: oxygen (43%), silicon (20%), magnesium (19%), iron (10%), various other metals & trace elements

Daily Motion: 13 degrees 12 minutes (average)

Rotational Period: Orbits the Earth; traverses the Zodiac in 27.3 days

Interesting Facts: Never shows the same face; goes through constant waxing or waning—the eight Lunar phases (New Moon to Full Moon and back again); reflects the light of the Sun

Astonishingly, although the Moon is 400 times smaller than the Sun, it is also 400 times closer, leading to the unlikely coincidence that they both appear the same size in our sky, a fact that allows eclipses to occur.

Although the Moon is a physical object, it also has an *astrological* character and governs many aspects of our world. These can be divided into several groups for each planet. Before you read on, try to imagine what kind of things (e.g., colours, plants, animals) are ruled by the Moon. Don't be afraid to use your intuition! Is the Moon silver or gold, for instance? Make notes in the box below. When you are ready, turn over the page and check at the full list. Did you guess right?

Fact File: The Moon In Astrology

Nature: feminine, cold, and wet, cooling, moist

Associated with: Monday, tides, fluctuation, breath, reflection, memory; milk, food, seeds, eggs

Colours: white, pale, silvery, transparent (glass)

Odours/Flavours: salty, bland, bitter, or mild and without flavour

Parts of the Body: breasts, stomach, lymphatics, hormones, the left eye

Appearance: fullness, short, fleshy hands, round face, fair of face

People/Occupations: midwives, nurses, mothers, sailors, anglers; gatherings, crowds

Places: dwellings, rivers, springs, lakes, seaports, seashores, caverns, deep shade

Animals: sea creatures, crustaceans, frogs, eels, otters, beavers, tortoises, snails, owls, cuckoos

Plants: soft, thick, shady, juicy leaves, grow quickly in watery places, e.g., cabbages, lettuces, onions, melons, cucumbers, mushrooms

Metals and Gemstones: silver, quartz crystal, moonstone, pearl

How did you do? Some of these connections and characteristics are straightforward, but many of them may seem random at first. They are not. Indeed, our ancestors in the early days of civilisation were well aware of these and used the wisdom they contain to great effect, helping them to survive and prosper, and ensuring that our generation would exist at all, against such great odds.

Let's look into these connections more deeply. The chief archetype of the Moon is the crab, because she (the Moon is feminine, remember) rules the zodiac sign of Cancer the crab. Crabs don't move in a straight line but go from side to side, akin to wandering. This is associated with the continually changing Moon phases ("What mood is she in?"), indicating the fluctuating emotions of life.

As the wandering mind, then, she has an abundance of thought about things (as images), bringing with it the gifts of premonition and intuition through a sensitivity to the environment and surroundings.

The Moon part in us likes to feel safe and protected, contained, and "within." This encourages growth and development. She is soft and tender, nourishing and nurturing—very much in the moment ("What does it feel like?"); she loves peace and is easily frightened.

The Moon is known for the beginning of things, like conception, where the seed meets the egg for example. To understand her nature, consider the role of a mother who generates and creates. When mother increases, so do all the things she involves herself with; but if mother decreases or diminishes, things follow. The goddess spirit in nature brings forth the productive principle. She can help perfect a life with growth.

When the sun is not shining and darkness falls, everything gets cooler; it is now that the Moon becomes apparent with the forming of airborne moisture and the process of condensation. In this way, the Moon rules the dew that covers all things before dawn and masses together to make bodies of water, such as dewponds.

The moon is the most obvious of the periodic or cyclic planets, constantly changing as she moves, and thus linked to the menstrual cycle, pregnancy, and childbirth.

☿ Mercury

Our second planet to unveil its secrets is Mercury. You may be asking why Mercury comes second in the list when it's nearest to the Sun, but don't worry for now—all will be revealed in the next section, when we uncover *The Divine Order*. First, let's get some facts about the physical planet.

Fact File: Mercury in the sky

Size: 3,030 miles in diameter

Distance: 36 million miles from the Sun; the closest planet, never farther than 27 degrees apart

Chemical Composition: metals (70%), silicates (30%)

Daily Motion: averages one degree, but when swift, can move almost two

Rotational Period: takes 88 days to orbit the Sun

Interesting Facts: visible every three months or so in the early morning, just before sunrise, or in the evening sky, just after sunset; as seen from Earth; appears to go in reverse for around 24 days; spends more time hidden by the bright rays of the Sun than any other planet

Now let's look at the wisdom hidden in this planet. Focus your mind on Mercury… What colours does it rule and what kind of places might be associated with it? Again, use your intuition, that deeply powerful sense that we all inherit from the generations upon generations past. Tune in to the spirit of Mercury and think what it is trying to tell us, then make notes in the box. When you are ready, look at the fact file overleaf.

Fact File: Mercury in Astrology

Nature: neutral, neither masculine nor feminine; changes according to what it is with; generally cold & dry

Associated with: Wednesday, sharp intelligence & understanding, trickery, deceit, cleverness, wit, logic, linguistics

Colours: multicoloured and complex; bluish grey, orange

Odours/Flavours: mixed & complex, a hodgepodge of blends but subtle and penetrating

Parts of the Body: belly, intestines, tongue, hands, fingers, shoulders, lungs, brain, nervous system, sense of hearing

Appearance: tall, thin; long arms, fingers, hands, and feet; a narrow face, forehead, thin lips and nose, sparkling eyes; full hair, small teeth

People/Occupations: merchants, secretaries, accountants, teachers, mail deliverers, bus and train drivers, printers, journalists, editors, rappers, software developers, gamers; liars, thieves

Places: shops, markets, schools, libraries, bus stops, train stations, traffic junctions

Animals: dogs, animals of quick sense, cunning creatures including serpents, hyenas, monkeys, apes, foxes, squirrels, weasels, and greyhounds; parrots, swallows, spiders, beetles, locusts, bees

Plants: beans, corn, walnuts, elder, hazel, aniseed, clove, coriander, oregano, ferns, reeds, aloe vera

Metals and Gemstones: quicksilver, platinum, coinage metals, agate

The name Mercury is speculated to derive from the same word that gives us "merchant," "market," and "mark" (in ancient Etruscan) and hence connects to trade, business, commerce, and communication, linking nicely with the apparent speed that the ancients observed this wanderer's movement and orbit. It is interesting too how in money markets, the word "current" (meaning flow and movement) also gives us "currency."

Mercury excels in forethought and intelligence and is a dab hand at making exchanges, "this for that, that for the other." Its sleight of hand and dexterous displays of skill can be deceptive in dealings, and it is known for lying, fickleness, untrustworthiness, frivolousness, and crooked morals.

Because of its clever hands and way of working with the mind, it is a weaver of stories, a persuasive interpreter with a view to a profit. Shrewd and cunning, it likes backhanders. Being two sided, unstable, and sometimes disturbed, it can flip on a sixpence and sell its story to the highest bidder, caring nothing of the outcome as it's moved on already.

No-one knows the contents of Mercury's soul, and it does not reveal these either; it can be a reliable friend sometimes but not always.

On the other hand, Mercury is proficient, charming, pleasant, encouraging, witty, ingenious, and inventive, with good manners and a beautiful voice! Mercury is also an eloquent guide, navigator, writer, speaker, interviewer, and poet.

♀ Venus

Venus is known to many as the morning or evening star, sparkling and bright. The third planet from the Earth, it often appears as one of the earliest lights in the night sky. Let's start with some facts.

Fact File: Venus in the sky

Size: 7,521 miles in diameter

Distance: 67 million miles from the Sun

Chemical Composition: carbon dioxide (96%), nitrogen (3.5%), trace elements

Daily Motion: about 1 degree, sometimes a little faster

Rotational Period: between the Earth and Sun; orbits the Sun in 225 days

Interesting Facts: retrograde phases, approximately every 18 months, last 43 days; alternates between the morning star (rising before the Sun) and the evening star (setting after the Sun).

Once again make some notes in the box below—how do you think Venus is going to be described?

What kind of ideas did you have? Are you getting better at these? Don't worry if not because all will become clear later on, and by the end of the book, you will be an expert! Let's find out more about Venus from an astrological point of view—the answers are on the next page!

Fact File: Venus in Astrology

Nature: feminine, nocturnal, cold, and moist

Associated with: Friday, beauty, luck, tranquillity, tolerance, generosity, devotion; pleasant objects and pastimes

Colours: green, straw coloured, pastel & milky colours

Odours/Flavours: sweet, greasy, aromatic; smells that arouse lust & pleasure, perfumes, pungent, agreeable, soft, ripe, delicious

Parts of the Body: sense of smell, lips, neck, throat, kidneys, genitalia

Appearance: handsome, an enticing body, beautiful eyes, glowing complexion, smooth skin, fair hair; cherry lips, eyes that wander, neat & stylish clothes

People/Occupations: musicians, singers, artists, jewellers, perfumiers, people involved in fashion, cosmetics, style, designers, decorators

Places: gardens, fountains, dressing rooms and bedchambers, adorned rooms, fashion and dancing schools, art galleries, places of entertainment & pleasure

Animals: dolphins, hens, sparrows, thrushes, nightingales, doves

Plants: rose, lilies, daffodils, apples, figs, peaches, apricots, valerian, thyme, strawberries, raspberries

Metals and Gemstones: copper, emerald, lapis lazuli

Representing desire and love and the emotions linked to relationships, friendship, and companionship, Venus generates cheerfulness, fun, laughter, favourable agreements, the enjoyment of life and a fondness for good food and drink, singing, dancing, and the beautiful arts. Indeed, she is a social planet, found at parties and gatherings, enjoying herself whilst also being gracious, polite, and well mannered. She is the fashion show, the current mode and season, the must-have, and the do-anything-for-it. As a matchmaker, she sees what works well together, be it in two people or in pairing food and drink. Venus wants to thrive and be prosperous and fruitful, delighting in recreation, sport, mirth, and jollity.

Venus is voluptuous in shape and form—the beauty in the eye of the beholder. She rules attraction and magnetism, sex, and love making, which naturally leads to harmonizing. Venus is the queen of pleasure, leisure, and indulgence, of course enjoying adornments—fancy jewellery, rings, decorations, garlands, or even a crown. She loves to give and receive gifts as well as focus on ownership and possession, with acquisition and wealth.

Can you identify the Venus within you? Do any of your friends or family typify the essence of this planet? Venus is the third planet in our list, and we now move on to the next planet, the Sun.

So now, having finished the three inner or *inferior* planets, we approach the central zone to see what it can tell us, before moving beyond to the outer or superior planets. (Note: a summary of these is in Addendum B.)

☉ The Sun

We have placed the Sun in the middle of this arrangement. And of course, we learned at school that the Sun is in the middle of the solar system. But some of the other planets seem out of order... why might that be? All will be revealed later on… As Hamlet notes, "there are more things in heaven and earth than are dreamt of in your philosophy."

For now here are some facts about the physical Sol, our nearest star.

Fact File: The Sun in the sky

Size: 865,000 miles in diameter—100 times as large as the Earth!

Distance: 93 million miles from the Earth

Chemical Composition: hydrogen (92%), helium (8%)

Daily Motion: just under one degree

Rotational Period: the Earth orbits every 365 days

Interesting Facts: is a star; from our perspective, its annual path across the sky creates a line called the *Ecliptic*, like a cosmic ring-road around which the other planets also seem to travel.

You know what to do by now—here's the box below for your ideas.

Fact File: The Sun in Astrology

Nature: masculine, rules the day, hot and dry, with heat predominant

Associated with: Sunday, light & glow, radiance, heat, warmth, dryness, the origin, and creation of life

Colours: yellow, gold, scarlet

Odours/Flavours: mixed sweet and sour, pungent, aromatic, richly spicy, bittersweet; nicely warming, myrrh, frankincense

Parts of the Body: head, heart, spine, right eye

Appearance: well-built body, warm, glowing complexion, large, round forehead; ruddy skin and large, roundish eyes, a large heart, a healthy & spirited constitution

People/Occupations: administrators, magistrates, constables, mayors, kings, princes, emperors, nobles; actors, MCs, people who work with minting gold, brass, copper

Places: palaces & royal courts, magnificent houses of which one is proud, stages, theatres, showrooms, halls, dining rooms, galleries, on a pedestal

Animals: lions, tigers, horses, rams, bulls, goats, glowworms, seals, crocodiles, peacocks, swans, cockerels

Plants: ash, palm, bay, cedar & citrus trees; sugar cane, vines, cinnamon, wheat & barley; plants and herbs with orange, yellow, or reddish flowers: sunflowers, saffron, and daisies

Metals and Gemstones: gold, ruby, amber, topaz

The sun gives us life; it is the creator of the world because we perceive everything around us—and create space and time—using its light. Thus, it is the All-Seeing Sun and nature's fire and intellectual light. Ancient astrologers referred to it as the organ of mental perception. Its light is the spiritual channel by which we can be en*light*ened, as we see later in the book.

Naturally, the Sun has authority and prestige over the other planets, like a leader or king; when in the sky, it has great power and nobody can look directly at its brilliant and overbearing rays. Anyone getting too close risks being incinerated—the further away, the safer. Remember the story of Icarus who flew to close to the Sun and fell to his doom when his wings melted.

As emperor of the stars, its nature is to be faithful but with a desire to rule and sway; its judgement is incomparable, and it boasts majesty and stateliness, industriousness, and strength. The sun is confident and commanding, affectionate, and humane to all. To be in the sun's light (at a good distance!) is to enjoy sumptuousness, magnificence, and a good heart.

♂ Mars

We now turn our attention to a planet that has figured large in our imaginations and literature, the so-called "Red Planet," Mars, with its famous red-tinged light and apparent signs of life via what were believed to be canals. Here are some facts for you.

Fact File: Mars in the sky

Size: 4,222 miles in diameter

Distance: 142 million miles from the Sun

Chemical Composition: iron dust, volcanic basalt rock; atmosphere of carbon dioxide (95%), nitrogen (2.5%), argon (1.5%)

Daily Motion: half a degree; its journey around the zodiac takes approximately 18 months

Rotational Period: orbits around the Sun in 687 days

Interesting Facts: retrograde phase lasts for 80 days, approximately every two years; has two moons, Phobos (fear) & Deimos (terror)

Mars appears in the sky with a red tint, a fact that did not go unnoticed by the ancients. This may have contributed to some of the aspects of the world that it rules. Have a think about what they might be, and make some notes in the box. Then read on and find out if you were right!

Fact File: Mars in Astrology

Nature: nocturnal, masculine, hot and dry

Associated with: Tuesday, courage, passion, desire, action, assertiveness, competitions, victors, fighters, sporting events, bodily strength & endurance, conquering; hot, hard, sharp, and red things, cutters, slicers, cleavers

Colours: fiery bright colours, blood red, yellow

Odours/Flavours: bitter, sharp, hot spiciness; aggressive smells like sulphur, ammonium

Parts of the Body: muscles in the body & head

Appearance: medium stature; lean, reddish complexion; curly, coarse, dry hair; sharp eyes with a piercing gaze & confident countenance

People/Occupations: military officers, soldiers, police; surgeons, doctors; blacksmiths, cooks, barbers, carpenters, martial artists

Places: forges, ovens, furnaces, weapons manufacturers, boxing rings, battlefields, arenas

Animals: rams, wolves, leopards, bears, hawks, vultures, ravens, wasps, mosquitoes, sharks, scorpions

Plants: stinging nettles, holly bushes, thistles, pines, chilli peppers, garlic, peppercorns, ginger, mustard, radishes

Metals and Gemstones: iron, jasper, garnet, magnetic lodestone

Mars' dryness and heat creates a splitting and divisive action, making it a difficult planet in its dynamic expression, with hardness and abruptness. It rules wars, violence, anger, quarrels, contentions, fighting, abuse, hatred, plundering, looting, banishment, and exile, bringing murder, bloodshed, and attacks of fever as well as physical ailments. Mars is found in ulcerations, burns, bites, and stings; it can torture and torment and create all manner of difficult circumstances, including inflammation, strokes, falls, and weak vision.

On the other hand, Mars also leads, commands, and campaigns with raw strength and an urge for victory. It is the mentally sharp youth who answers quickly, exerts, and has hardiness, haste, and daring. Mars is a disputant, takes orders from nobody, acts thoughtlessly, and will not stay put.

Mars is indifferent to his effects: if hired by evil, he works violence to evil ends. But when hired by good, he works equally hard for worthy purposes, thus having the unshakeable capacity to hew down as well as build up. Mars forges a purpose—he surrounds and upholds a well-disposed character.

Because Mars is a superior planet, he travels on the outer side of the Earth and pulls all things away from the centre. Whereas earlier planetary forces are *centripetal,* Mars acts *centrifugally,* and his sense of push and pull has a desire to fulfil, even though it may be held down by the weight of earthly life and the gravity of existence, potentially making Mars the instigator of war and strife as it attempts to assert itself to reach completion.

Once again, look inside to see what aspects of your life and character are ruled by Mars. Is he having a positive or a negative effect on you at the moment? Now we continue with the next of the superior planets, the king of the gods, Jupiter.

♃ Jupiter

Jupiter is a huge planet with its famous "red spot," and when astonished by something, our natural phrase may be "By Jove!" using its alternate name. Anything this size must surely have both a large influence on us and also plenty to teach us, so it will be an interesting study. First, as usual, let's look at its physical attributes to get an idea of how amazing this world is.

Fact File: Jupiter in the sky

Size: 88,800 miles in diameter; the largest planet

Distance: 484 million miles from the Sun

Chemical Composition: a gaseous "balloon-like" planet with over 60 moons

Daily Motion: 0.2 degrees; it takes about twelve years to finish a course through the zodiac

Rotational Period: 10 hours; moves on its axis very fast

Interesting Facts: goes retrograde for four months annually; sometimes brighter than Mars; surface has extreme weather patterns

Jupiter is clearly the king of the planets, but how does it impact on our world? What influences does it bring to bear? Make notes in the box below about the things we might relate to Jupiter, and then check the fact file.

Fact File: Jupiter in Astrology

Nature: diurnal, masculine, hot & moist

Associated with: Thursday, luck; completion, the good things in life; smooth, shiny things; fruitfulness, givers of life; thunder & lightning, growth (including embryos)

Colours: purple, blue, burgundy

Odours/Flavours: non-offensive, pleasantly enjoyable, fragrant, scented

Parts of the Body: liver, thighs, feet; parts of the right side

Appearance: a pleasant figure, upright stance, full thighs and strong legs, an oval face, soft hair, a large belly, long feet

People/Occupations: politicians, town councillors, judges, court professions, bishops, priests; university lecturers, professors, chancellors, governors, students, travellers, pilgrims, publishers

Places: places of worship, mountains, valleys, great heights, courts of justice, universities, laboratories

Animals: stags, oxen, elephants, dragons, storks, snipes, larks, eagles, partridges, pheasants, peacocks, whales

Plants: cherry, mulberry, oak, olive, almond, pear, beech; nutmeg, rhubarb, mint

Metals and Gemstones: tin, pewter, amethyst, marble, limestone

Think of Jupiter like a great gift of prosperity, bringing relief from troubles and release from bonds. Sincere and truthful, just and understanding, he conveys uprightness, endurance, unification, and reverence.

Well disposed, inspiring, high minded, and devout, he desires to do good and benefit all with glorious, honourable, and virtuous deeds. Deeply connected to religion, Jupiter has authority and is god-fearing, modest, and pious in worship, such that giving praise is natural and good.

A lucky spirit that gives charitably, Jupiter brings comfort. He is prosperous, successful, and dignified, with a magnificence that delights and an indulgence full to the brim with fun, joy, and laughter. He is also wise, offering good, trusted counsel and is an expert on law and a fair judge. He must, however, be wary of a potential for recklessness or undue haste, as enthusiasm can get carried away. He can be hypocritical and careless.

Overall, Jupiter is expansive, benevolent, large, and lavish, seeking and creating the abundant good life, while aligning with moral and religious law and righteousness. As well as luxury and wealth, he can also practice sobriety and temperance.

Our journey through this space is nearly at an end but we have one more planet to come, and what a planet it is! Saturn has one of the most recognisable shapes, and if asked to draw a planet, many children will instinctively reproduce the classic ringed planet in an instant.

♄ Saturn

Saturn, with its notable rings, is the farthest visible planet seen with the naked eye and the second largest. It appears to have a cold and distant light, with a greyish quality. Let's find out more…

Fact File: Saturn in the sky

Size: 74,900 miles in diameter

Distance: 886 million miles from the Sun

Chemical Composition: hydrogen (75%), helium (25%), methane, ammonia, water ice (traces)

Daily Motion: 0.03 degrees; 12 degrees per year

Rotational Period: takes 29.46 years to orbit the Sun

Interesting Facts: viewed through a telescope, its ice rings can be seen; once per year it retrogrades for about 5 months

For the final time, please now make notes in the box below about the influences that Saturn might have on our world. Then check in the fact file on the next page.

Fact File: Saturn in Astrology

Nature: diurnal, masculine, cold & dry

Associated with: Saturday, solitude, loneliness, barrenness, a rock, heaviness, problems, restrictions, finality

Colours: black, leaden grey, dark green, yellow

Odours/Flavours: bitter, sour, sharp, unpleasant, acetic; offensive odours

Parts of the Body: spleen, skin, teeth, bones

Appearance: stooped, lean, cold, and dry, swarthy, dark eyes, lank belly, thin legs, crooked shoulders or knees; hard, a rugged look, well weathered, time worn, white/grey hair, wrinkled skin

People/Occupations: miners, plumbers, chimney sweeps, stonemasons, monks, retirement helpers, odd jobbers, beggars, funeral directors, grave diggers, animal handlers, stablehands

Places: frozen ground, graveyards, ruins, dens, sinks, wells, deserts, deep dark forests

Animals: cats, mice, moles, dogs, toads, reptiles, hogs, tortoises, bats, ostriches, blackbirds, robins

Plants: yew, cypress, willow trees, hemp, tamarisk, capers, cumin, poppies, ferns, moss, nightshade, hemlock, boxwood

Metals and Gemstones: lead, onyx, jet, obsidian

As the outermost planet, Saturn is seen as a boundary or wall. It tends to bring problems, endings, or death and restricts through hardness (like the frozen ground of winter).

Saturn represents the aging process; as the body dries out, it becomes less flexible, so its archetype is an old man with a long white beard, scythe, and hourglass. The scythe represents ploughing, farming, the cultivation of land, and building—the effort of working with the hands for long hours, slavishly. The hourglass represents the restriction of time; we are only in this body and life for a set duration. Death awaits, so Saturn rules corruption, decay, and rotting or falling apart, suffering, delays, fear, anxieties, sorrows, dejection, and adversity.

Saturn is found in disgraced people with a bad reputation, misers and the resented, lamenters and the conceited. Saturn is long in thought but of few words, being obtuse, stubborn, deliberate, coercing, confining, suspicious, selfish, and not loving the good in anyone.

On the other hand, Saturn earns genuine respect and self-esteem, becoming wise and experienced through perseverance. Reliable, responsible, duty bound, and obligating, Saturn is deep rather than shallow. A good Saturn is successful in its labours, through being studious and solicitous, and in all actions, austere.

Where do these rulerships come from?

You may be wondering how we are able to list so many examples for each of these planets! And where do they come from? Some make immediate sense. For example, the planet Mars has a traditionally warlike character, so it is naturally associated with fighting or fire. Look at the occupations listed on page 29, and see if can you make connections between each of them and either heat or blades.

For another example, take a look at the animals listed under the Sun... what possible connection is there between crocodiles, goats, and peacocks? Well, for a start, imagine a scene with crocodiles—what are they doing? Most of the time, they are sitting around, waiting for lunch to come along, *sunning* themselves. This is perhaps because they are cold blooded, which means they rely upon, and are ruled by, the warmth of the Sun. For their own part, peacocks strut around, confidently in control of the garden, with a vast shimmering display akin to the multicoloured rays of the sun. But how could *goats* possibly be connected? Well, have you ever tried to tell a goat what to do? If so, you'll have discovered that they are self ruling, the king of their own field, another trait of the Sun.

These are just examples to help explain what might be a mysterious and confusing list at first. However, if you persevere and work with them, they will gradually start to become clear. Don't rush it—take your time. Be creative in your understanding and interpretations, and they will enhance your understanding of *The Divine Order* and why it is so.

Now, a common question is who exactly decided these and when were they worked out. One possible origin is from an integrated system of correlations used in Ancient Mesopotamia (and quite possibly a lot earlier). This was written down by the Roman philosopher, physician, and surgeon, Galen of Pergamon, born in the year 129 AD. He wrote about

these links in the sense of "correspondences." These are succinctly defined by Fred Gettings in his *Dictionary of Astrology* (1985) as, "the ... hidden relationships between natural forms and spiritual causes, or between the microcosm and the macrocosm."

In fact, according to the ancient wisdom, *everything* on Earth—every object, creature, and feeling—has a correspondence with the celestial heavens above, so that the spiritual can be read through the physical. All phenomena, as experienced by the five senses and interpreted in the human mind, are embedded in a network of interconnectedness and meaning, sometimes known as "the great chain of being" (which you can read more about in the sequel to this book!). In large part, these hidden correspondences are profoundly archetypal and metaphorical in their nature.

Put another way, everything in our world is governed or ruled by one of the seven planets introduced in this chapter. As we shall see later on in the book, this knowledge or awareness is key and will help inform our everyday actions, thoughts, and feelings.

The planets in our life

So, we have now started to get to know the planets and their characters really quite well. Can you see them in the world around you and recognise them as dynamic parts of your personality and those of your friends and family? Of course, many mysteries remain to be explained: What is *The Divine Order*? Why is it *divine*? Where does the order come from? And perhaps most importantly, how does it affect me? All these questions and more will be answered in the next chapter, *The Divine Order*!

4: The Divine Order

The Sun—Shining a light on the true order of nature

☉

You may have noticed that the list of planets in Part 3 starts with the Moon rather than the Sun and omits some, including the Earth! There are other oddities and differences from the "normal" perspective that we learnt at school and know so well. To explain these differences, we now introduce the fundamental point of this book, namely *The Divine Order*.

So, just what *is* this Divine Order? It is an ancient way of looking at the solar system, which, when mapped out, parallels the body, mind, soul, and spirit—the entire human experience. When combined with the planetary correspondences identified in the previous chapter, it will shed light on many aspects of our everyday life as well as give concrete suggestions for how to diagnose and solve problems.

First, let's see where *The Divine Order* comes from. Then, we give more details. Finally, we must show what it means for us in theory, before moving on to the all-important practical side in Part 5.

Deriving *The Divine Order*

To understand where The Divine Order comes from, we need to use four steps. Let's take them one by one.

Step 1: From geocentric to heliocentric…

The wisdom this book reveals is based on an ancient ordering of the planets that stretches back more than 5,000 years. The great early civilisations of Babylonia and Mesopotamia saw themselves at the centre or hub of their reality as they stood on the Earth and observed the visible planets orbiting them at different speeds. The planets' orbits made repeating patterns, and this helped them to develop the time system we know today (seconds, minutes, hours, days, months, years, etc.).

This belief in a cosmological model and the power of the imagination evolved further through the Greek and Roman Empires all the way through the mediaeval era, but remained largely unchanged.

This perspective, placing the Earth at the centre, is known as the *geocentric viewpoint*, where *geo* is a prefix meaning "*Earth*," also used in words like *geo*logy and *geo*graphy. *Centric* just means it's in the middle of things. This was the accepted way of understanding the cosmos and our place within it for millennia: the seven heavens, the crystal firmament.

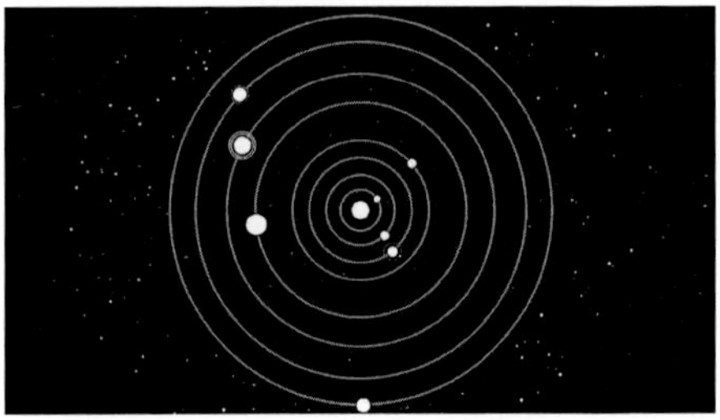

However, there was a problem with this viewpoint that began to emerge with the Renaissance and the development of science. The growth of trade and travel put Europeans into contact with peoples increasingly further east, including nomads who had inhabited deserts for generations, having to rely on the stars for navigation in the absence of any fixed landmarks. These peoples had, by necessity, developed mathematics and there was an explosion of this in the West, including geometry, algebra, and calculus. (It is enlightening that many terms from maths come from oriental languages—algebra is from the Arabic *al-jebr* meaning "reuniting broken parts" and even the concept of nothing, "zero" comes from the Sanskrit, *sunya-m* meaning "empty place or desert.")

The honing of glass lenses and consequent development of the telescope combined with mathematics to begin the mapping of the planets in terms of orbits. It was realised that the odd dance of some of the planets—which was very hard to describe with a mathematical equation—could be greatly simplified by placing the Sun at the centre.

Hence, what you probably learned at school—that it is a *fact* that the Sun is at the centre of our solar system, followed by Mercury and Venus, and then the Earth with its Moon orbiting around it—is the scientific standpoint in place since the work of Copernicus in 1542 and Galileo in the early 1600s. This understanding is known as the *heliocentric viewpoint,* where *helio* means "sun." (Indeed, the element *helium* is named after the Sun because it was first discovered there in the light spectrum before being produced on the Earth.)

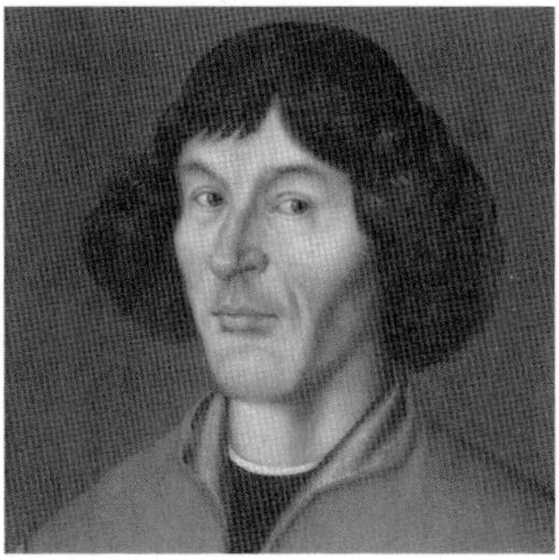

Work by Kepler and Newton confirmed that this arrangement of orbits around the Sun rather than the Earth—heliocentric rather than geocentric—made sense and ultimately led to the theory of gravity. This was the starting point of the scientific revolution and prioritising of objectivity that continues to this day.

Step 2: From heliocentric to humanocentric

This book, however, will take a different route. Because we are focussing on the human world, and because humans are (currently) based firmly on the Earth, there must be value and meaning in returning to see things from our viewpoint, a return to a more subjective way of thinking.

Does this require a return to geocentrism? No, we will be more subtle than this in favour of what we term (for now) as "humanocentrism." Of course, if we place our human world at the centre of the cosmos, and because we are standing on the Earth, it includes geocentrism—but the focus is different.

So, are we denying the scientific wisdom, Newton, gravity, and all? NO! In fact, even in heliocentrism, the sun is not at the centre of the universe or even the Milky Way galaxy—if the universe is infinite, which is possible, it doesn't even have a centre!

In fact, putting the Sun at the centre of the solar system is a great benefit as it helps to make the mathematical equations simpler, and is hence regarded as more fundamental and useful, but which is no more *true* than any other viewpoint (see Einstein's theory of relativity, in which all viewpoints are equally true...). For furthering our material knowledge of the universe and technology, this scientific simplicity is helpful and we do not want or need to undermine it. However, it is not the only interpretation, and indeed, given the condition of the globe especially in terms of ecology, one might say that taken alone, it may not be the best.

The geocentric—or better, humanocentric—interpretation is just different, and one that informs us as humans on a living planet, so this is the one we will adopt here.

(And the fact that we and the planet form a holistic living entity mean that ultimately, even humanocentrism isn't quite complete, so Book 2 will extend this to *Gaia*centrism...)

Step 3: From 10 to 7 planets...

The list in Part 3 comprised seven planets—some are missing, including Uranus, Neptune, and possibly Pluto, depending on whether current thinking makes this a planet or not.

Why have we used just these seven for this book? Well, because we are helio- or humanocentric, we will treat the Earth as a given—we can't see it in the sky and it doesn't move, so it's not included as a sphere. Remember that the ancients regarded the Earth as stationary and unmoving at the centre of the universe. The seven planets chosen are the only ones visible from the Earth with the naked eye, without modern technology.

Uranus was one of the first of the "new" planets, discovered by Sir

William Herschel in 1781, using the powerful telescope he had developed. This was one of the great scientific turning points, taking human knowledge and awareness beyond what we could experience directly with our own natural senses, and implying the existence of many worlds beyond our own. Neptune and Pluto, as well as their own moons, were to follow. However, it is just the seven astronomical bodies contained in *The Divine Order* that are directly visible and are hence the ones that can influence us. However, these wandering and dancing little points in the sky are much more than just pieces of rock and gas!

Step 4: From planets to spheres...

The Divine Order consists of "spheres" rather than just points. Why is this? Well, planets are just dots in the sky, distant and remote lumps of rock or gas, whereas spheres are multidimensional and enclose and envelop us, becoming "spheres of influence" in the mind.

Moreover, these spheres are concentric and nested—like Russian *Matryoshka* dolls, they also cover and envelop each other, stretching outwards in the cosmos, with us—humans—at their centre.

Why are they ordered like this?

So now we know that *The Divine Order* has us in the middle, surrounded by seven ever-larger concentric spheres, each governed by one of the seven visible planets. But why are they in this order?

Let's return to our collective ancient ancestors, those early humans who relied entirely on their senses to survive and propagate the species (or we wouldn't even be here!). Remember, for them, the planets were like living creatures moving independently in an otherwise fixed firmament. And what they noticed was that not just the direction of travel varied, but also the apparent speed of the planets was different. How could they explain this? One answer could be that the fastest ones were clearly the nearest, and hence had the greatest influence on us.

How is this speed measured? Because the planets are seen as spheres, their movement is circular and measured in degrees (see the planetary fact files for details). Of course, this is just the *apparent* speed as seen from our particular viewpoint on the Earth, but that is what is important to us.

Clearly the Moon is the fastest of all, moving 13 degrees per day. Of course, this means it can perform a complete rotation in 28 days (360 degrees divided by 13), giving us our month. Mercury—known for its speed—moves around 1 degree per day, so it comes second. And so on, up through the seven planets until we reach Saturn, which moves at the snail's pace of nine days per degree, but which nevertheless has a big influence on us. And that gives us our *Divine Order*:

The Moon > Mercury > Venus > The Sun > Mars > Jupiter > Saturn

The Divine Order in seven spheres

So, the seven visible wandering planets give us the seven great spheres of influence, rotating around us, and ordered by apparent speed—*The Divine Order*. We have already cited Mercury for its speed, but each of the seven spheres gives us an archetype—including all the influences seen in the Astrological Fact Files in Part 3.

And, not only are they ordered by *distance* and *speed*, but that order itself provides a natural or divine *sequence*. This gives us a direction to travel when performing actions or making plans, and holds great promise. The order is as follows:

feelings > logic > relationships > light > actions > growth > law

You may already be starting to see how this natural order can manifest itself in our daily life, not just explaining successes and failures, but also acting as a guide and diagnostic tool. (In Part 6, we focus on this aspect with some specific case studies and examples.)

We have already learned about the physical planets and the aspects of the world they rule, and now it is time to see how they influence our imagination, feelings, behaviour, emotions, psychology, and all other aspects of human life. So let's introduce each of the seven archetypical planetary spheres in turn, and help restore our place in the universe.

In order to explain the influences of these spheres on us, we can consider them akin to the phases of human life, from babyhood to old age and beyond. Each sphere, as well as its archetype (e.g., the Moon rules feelings) is also closely linked to one particular age (e.g., the Moon is babyhood, from birth to age 4).

However, it is vital to understand that as we stand at the centre of these seven concentric spheres, *each* of them will influence *each* stage of our lives, so the Moon will continue to have an impact throughout the whole of our lifetimes, and understanding that impact will allow us to spot, diagnose, and resolve problems, as well as find balance and joy in the benefits of being a particular age. To highlight these age/stage links, we will describe the seven spheres, in their *Divine Order*, as stages in life, but remember this is for illumination only, and whatever age you are, you will be under the influence of all seven, reflecting the fractal nature of the cosmos.

☽ The sphere of feelings (the Moon)

The first level of consciousness: Feeling through your senses

According to the ancient way, the Moon orbits the Earth like a sphere, perfect in shape and movement—a boundary between the terrestrial sphere and the rest of the celestial heavens. This is also a sphere of the imagination.

As the first sphere, the Moon sets the scene and the beginnings of who we are, encasing us in a realm called the sublunary sphere. Underneath is where all material life is created, imperfect and impermanent. An apt metaphor is an ocean seashell with a fractal spiral shape. Inside is a space for life to exist, enclosed by its own movement and gradual growth. The Moon is the closest to nature, being its nurturer and carer, breathing in the *pneuma* of the great spirit.

You can follow your own emotional cycle within a one-month period. At New Moon, hidden feelings are generated from the unconscious mind and realm of dreams. These gather themselves together and grow over fourteen days to become obvious and conscious at the Full Moon, when they are "bought into the light." After this, the lunar disc wanes and loses its light. That moment of awakening is gradually integrated into your life.

From an ancient viewpoint, all life comes through the Moon to be born. Therefore, the Moon rules fertility and procreation cycles in the animal kingdom. When a newborn is formed out of the soul, it experiences pure awareness with no concept of space or time. All being well, the primary needs to survive comfortably are provided: food, love, cuddles, care, warmth, and safety. Gradually, over repeating lunar cycles and the progress of time, the first level of consciousness begins to form, taking four years to complete before evolving into the next sphere (Mercury). It is in this Moon-sphere development that the earliest memories of life are stored, closely connected to the unconscious mind.

This means from the moment of birth up until the first four years of life, it is vital to create favourable conditions for development. You need a good experience of life to encourage healthy growth and development of personality. In psychology, it is known as growth related patterns.

The abundance of imagery arising from the unconscious mind suggests readiness of invention and development. Because there is a constant and never-ending flow (like a babbling stream) into the conscious mind in the first few years of life, you become familiar with your responses and reactions, eventually becoming comfortable with all that is happening in

each moment. The enlightened teachers, lamas, and gurus tell us that the flow of thoughts never stops; they are in a constant movement, and we should not try to stop but just observe it. It is through disciplined mind training of meditation that you can see the difference between awareness and the flow of thinking. And we will be introducing some meditations later on in this book!

At birth, you had no boundary to the world outside and perceived everything with clarity and luminosity, because you hadn't defined or objectified anything in your new world. Do you remember peeking over the swaddling blanket into infinity? Did it feel safer to stay warm in a cot, or comfy in mother's embrace?

Everything below the Moon is mutable and contingent because it is the planet that governs thoughts as they arise. If you only had the Moon from which to divine your life, you would not know what was going to happen next!

Essentially, the Moon is like a funnel or focussing lunar lens that channels all the other planets as they flow down to the sublunary sphere, where the Earth lies, and where you receive all their influences. If the Moon is unhappy or obstructed, she won't be as effective in channelling the other planets.

All life is born through, into, and under the Moon. To be born under the Moon is to take on a physical body and the sense of being and existing. The eternal soul creates the body around itself, and birth occurs. This is the necessary precursor for an earthly life.

Because the Moon receives all influences from the other planets as they descend to Earth, she is the repository of habitual patterns. These can range from eating (under- or overeating; preferring or shunning foods) to internal mind patterns we develop, for example, saying to yourself, "They don't like me" before you have even got to know someone.

Statements such as "I can't do this" may be based on past experiences which in fact have no grounding in the present. A good example of this might be a child ready to start walking who says, "I don't want to walk", when he or she obviously can and needs to take the opportunity to overcome this challenge. This is the effect of the Moon, as it reviews the memories in the container of being, and makes statements based on what was remembered, rather than what is now. This can be a major problem for many, a hurdle holding people back from free-flowing happiness. Later, in Parts 5 and 6, we show you how to reset past patterns and memory loops to redefine your link to the divine creation of the present, and thus regenerate your creativity.

☿ The sphere of logic (Mercury)

The Second Level of Consciousness: Learning to be Rational

So far, you have found your geocentric centre and the pure awareness from which everything emanates, encased by the first sphere of the Moon. Around age 7, then, the individual starts to reach out to learn more about the world around, leaving behind the Moon (having developed habitual patterns) to move into the next sphere, Mercury. This is the domain of the school years, in which learning features as a central theme, and it lasts until age 14.

It is the natural extension of the Moon because, when growing up, we learn to communicate in speech and writing; it can be sensed in the space around you as Mercury rules the hands and fingers—the part of the body often used to communicate via pens, pencils, keyboards, or smartphones. Language has a basis in the logic that is grammar, and this is emphasised in the Mercury sphere.

The formation of character and personality via the early school years is when you start to gain the idea of speech: how to reply to people, conduct a conversation, and make opinions or ideas understood. In effect, you start to see yourself as a thinking mind, developing and moving away from the pure eternal awareness of birth. This formation of a personalised and unique mind is the essence of Mercury. It is the first stages of development of the ego: quite literally "I think therefore I am."

Mercury is youthful. It is still the beginning of life with zest and spark, moving away from mother and the cot into the world around it to exchange its ideas and start integrating with the world. Mercury is facts and figures.

In the age of the Mercury sphere, you no longer pick up food with fingers but use a knife and fork in planned coordination. You no longer finger paint but learn to use a brush; don't just scribble but use the alphabet and cursive writing; don't just listen to music but read the stave and configure the notes.

Above all, Mercury is the sphere of logic. In this way, it is quite the opposite of the Moon sphere, which relates to feelings and sensations. They are both necessary and equal in importance, and balance is the key.

In terms of psychotherapeutic context, Mercury is the sphere containing any issues surrounding school and education. In those early years of learning, anything traumatic and difficult could be retained as a memory that might need to be worked out. Beliefs formed now can affect adulthood. As with all the spheres, you must understand the sequence in which the challenge occurs—careful contemplation and recall will help remove perceived blockages and loosen up the movement of consciousness to manifest what you want in life.

The Mercury sphere is where decisions are made; we look at options and come up with ideas. Does your Mercury help you construct thoughts carefully or is it the type that streams out a flow of consciousness? While clear, crisp, decisive, thinking is one of life's greatest gifts, we don't all have those gifts, so becoming more mindful of speech helps gain wisdom.

Mastery of the mind through meditation is the goal of the second sphere of Mercury because if you can use the breath to still the mind, you can start understand its working to build your seven-sphere cosmology.

To fully move into Mercury, then, means absorbing the understanding of memory (Moon) and what one learns about life (Mercury) from one's personal past history as a reflection process (Moon).

♀ The sphere of relationships (Venus)

The Third Level of Consciousness: Learning to Trust

Part of growing up is adolescence, ruled by the Venus sphere. This phase of life and personality development lasts around eight years, from 14 to 22. It begins with the *tween*, between child and young adult, where hormonal changes begin the ripening and maturing of emotional nature.

However, the teenager, becoming more sensitive, starts to discover how they are different from everybody else, especially parents and families. They can retreat into their own world and room, leading to potential difficulties establishing relationships with others outside their immediate circle.

Powerful emotions such as love, desire, anger, and jealousy start to be felt now for the first time, and the young person must learn how to cope with and integrate these emotions into their personality.

This is where the softer, gentler experience of childhood begins to give way, replaced by an assured poise and confidence. The Mercury and Moon spheres—highly adaptable—give way to a discriminating appraisal of the situations and people around. All the gathered experiences of childhood are analysed, balanced, and assimilated to help develop a new groundwork of taste and behaviour.

It is a stage of questioning and determining self-worth, self-esteem and self-value. And are you able to transmit your intelligence and communicate your mental developments across to others successfully?

This sphere balances sensation and accommodating yourself and others in a harmonic way. It is about defining how you will eventually want to relate to others. Friendships really start developing in this sphere, and situations intensify as you discover what you really need. And as you share intimacy with others, trust becomes all-important.

Sometimes things can get somewhat unstable, when the sensation and balance of Venus swings across its axis as you get to know yourself better—a form of trial and error. The rebel you might find situations where you are estranged: "Oh well I seem to have fallen out with this. What can I do? Oh well, I'm still me, and (hopefully) I still have other people to be around and things to do." This is the beginning of self-valuing.

The resulting teenage anxieties of how to relate can be overwhelming for some young people, and the added input of social media also reduces the sense of privacy, adding increased exposure to the public eye or judgement by contemporaries; the result is a constant urge to comparing yourself to others.

Sexuality is deeply involved at this point of development, because now you are familiarising yourself with an adult body for the first time and need to answer the questions: "What's this for?" "and What does this do?"

This is the age when the young person learns to fall in love, not only with a chosen partner but also art, culture, and aesthetic ideals, swayed by trends and fashions and, more importantly, the impact of crushes, fads, and crazes. It is about integrating into the accepted social norms and finding groups with similar conduct and methods of social relationship.

Overall, it is learning to fit in with the rest of society and cooperate with others; and in this way, preparing for marriage, long-term love, relationships, and later years.

☉ The sphere of light (The Sun)

The Fourth Level of Consciousness: Becoming Measured and Balanced

This phase of development begins at around age 21 and lasts for 20 years. Now, the young adult is fully formed and has become the youth who takes on the world and attempts to shine in their own light. It is a coming of age, which some people refer to as the "key to the door." In some parts of the world, the age of 21 is recognised as a turning point of maturity. The youth remains pliable and can be shaped by influential people or situations. Only in later spheres do things become rigid and inflexible.

This is the time to set up basic assumptions of how the world is and set down roots for further development. For many, it is the start of the material world, where careers are chosen, routines and regular patterns developed, and society's expectations met. There is a sense of settling down and establishing identity to discover and develop your life's purpose. This leads to a justification of existence: "I am here to be this or do that." You are seeking to earn a place in society, by the shining light of your Sun sphere.

A large part of how the Sun sphere emanates is due to the development of the earlier three. If you have had difficulties and challenges, it is quite likely that certain parts of personality are not shining through enough to bolster and support the Sun in its need to create a radiant individual or personality.

Painful and difficult situations can arise that need to be dealt with, particularly around the age of 28 and 29, as you come to terms with any blocks and delays to the previous development you had wished for. (In Astrology, this is known as *the Saturn return.*) The Sun sphere stage is where you must decide what kind of person you are going to be and how to fulfil the promise shown so far by the other spheres.

Ultimately, it is about being vital and dynamic—the individualising principle in nature,where "the One" out of all really starts to show. As the solar orb lights up the sky and gives light, so the individual develops an ego identity, self-illuminating and emanating radiance and the power of selfhood.

As the light is complete and surrounds us—as do the heavens—we are linked by radiance to every segment of the surrounding sky. All the powers of light within our universe have a correspondence in our soul, so it is good for the individual to affirm the celestial environment, along with all the spheres of the imagination.

There are separate parts within the larger whole; with the Sun at the midpoint of the journey, the three spheres on either side have a path in the personality and a dynamic characteristic that converges on the light at the centre. When the individual awakens to the radiance within themselves, they are drawn to this; the 20-year phase is all about finding a personal centre from which to grow.

As an individual, you exist at a fulcrum point of observation, seeing in both directions, understanding why you are like you are; it is vital at this stage to take the time to fix and solve any problems, especially anything remaining from the previous stages (spheres).

The goal of this phase is to fully recognise innate potential and become your own source of light within a personal sphere of influence. At this stage of life, you have tested, become experienced, and learned about yourself through the Moon, Mercury, and Venus. Yet to happen are Mars, Jupiter, and Saturn—ultimately the goal is to be **one**, and each sphere contributes to making this complete unity of self.

♂ The sphere of actions (Mars)

The Fifth Level of Consciousness: Gaining Potency and Outbound Action

This sphere of life is governed by Mars, starting at around 41 years old and lasting until the age of 56. You are now maturing, so the consolidation of power begins, along with a desire to act out and focus energy on specific goals or achievements.

As personality stabilises after 20 years of Sun-sphere influence, new forces are set in motion. There is a more energetic influence and a dynamic element in which you begin to assert leadership. Sometimes that can be physical, demanding strenuous effort as ambitions take control.

Conflicts can continue to arise, and stress can also manifest, particularly if you have not yet found a niche in life and are still searching for a place to plant your flag. Individuals who have developed the previous four spheres successfully now gain confidence and momentum to be bolder in their actions, establishing and firming up their place in the world.

Here are some typical phrases from someone undergoing the sphere of actions that is governed by Mars. Do any of them resonate with your own experience? Do you ever find yourself or your friends and family saying them?

- "I have this to say to the world."
- "I am certain of this, as my life experience tells me to push it forward."
- "From all my gathered experiences, I get frustrated and angered by this in society. I want to be able to do something about it."
- "I can be a leader too; I can take action to get results."

These and other similar phrases and feelings are the classic signs of someone in this phase of their life, the phase of expressing potency and outbound action, when it is necessary to take personal initiative to push for recognition or identity. Of course, this can involve struggle and pain. However, the Mars sphere is out to conquer and overcome the limitations of being human if possible, so, it sets a target and strides forward regardless. It may result in a passionate urge to fight for the desired object or status so that the Sun and three other previous spheres can act in a complete movement that justifies the cause.

Are you at this stage and in this sphere? Do you feel any of these forces acting on you? Are you happy about them or do you want to change things? If so, remember it is always possible, and the activities in the next part of the book will, we hope, help you to achieve this.

♃ The sphere of growth (Jupiter)

The Sixth Level of Consciousness: Expanding in Truth

This sphere is the pinnacle of life; it is represented by the age span 56 to 68, although of course this sphere, as with all the others, has a continual impact and influence on the lives of everyone of whatever age. Jupiter is its ruling planet, so it includes reflection on your original purpose and also possible recognition and honours.

There is now an overall expansion of personality and the dynamic characteristics developed until now. This stage of development is dependent on how the other spheres have been completed; if you have developed a solidity and groundedness, you will reap the rewards of your efforts.

Jupiter is the sphere of wisdom, and there can be a development of faith and philosophy of life—the things you believe in—at this maturing stage of adulthood. The growth of enterprises and business can involve travel, teaching, and significant assessments of validity. There is a strong focus on meaning and meaningfulness as you ask what kind of person you are now, and what the future might now hold.

The solid direction of life followed so far may make it difficult to change direction, but there is plenty of room for modifying attitudes and assumptions so that deeper beliefs concerning the purpose of life can be discovered and enjoyed.

Here are some typical phrases from someone undergoing the Sphere of Growth that is governed by Jupiter. Do any of them resonate with your own experience? Do you ever find yourself or your friends and family saying them?

- "What is my true purpose in life having got this far?"
- "I believe in this, and I want you to know it too."
- "I am defining my morals and ethics clearly now, for all to see."
- "I would like to show you my philosophy."
- "I believe the world needs to move in this direction."
- "I can't stand politics" OR "I must get involved in politics."

Jupiter shows the unfolding of the higher abstract mind as the centrifugal force pulls you outwards further towards God and the meaning of life. This natural growth of the developing psyche involves your personal feelings and social responses.

This sphere helps coordinate the others and assimilate them into your belief system. Jupiter is a collective order that determines individual behaviour and is mindful of the deeper implications of personality development within the whole order.

Now, this far-seeing sphere encompasses much within the bounds of what is possible for you to achieve. You can enjoy optimistic faith and nature's abundance, with more capacity for positive thinking, prestige, and prosperity. Within this sphere of development, luck is fused with purposefulness; if you do what you believe in and put your faith into something, good fortune will result.

♄ The sphere of law (Saturn)

The Seventh Level of Consciousness: Toeing the Line

This is the seventh and last stage of development, ruled by Saturn, the planet of old age. The sphere begins at the age of 68 and lasts until the age of 98 (when the cycle starts again from the Moon sphere). It brings the realisation that age has its limits, things slow down, and there is a natural decline.

Reaching the end of natural growth, your hope is to have forged a well-defined mountain pathway to the top, giving attainment and completion. Conversely it can be a rut, leading toward the grave, where tiredness and exhaustion dominate, along with a feeling that the *gravitas* of life has become too heavy to bear.

This fear enhances the understanding of what it is to have a sound and mature judgement of others and situations; it is also when your self-discipline becomes dominant as you place boundaries in life due to what remains still achievable.

However, if the other spheres have been difficult to complete or encompass, the individual at this last sphere can verge on depression and sadness—the healing has not been done.

Ultimately, this is the phase of self-mastery, and by now, you should know the difference between right and wrong. If there is suffering, you will have a good idea for what purpose you must endure it. This adds to your ability to function as an authority in the social sphere. If you have proved your ability to govern yourself, you are fit to govern others. You now act in your own right and impose an order developed through your own path of individualising. This is a distinctive ego structure that has been internalised.

This last sphere helps you shape society as society originally shaped you. Upholding the accepted laws and ways of being ensures the continuity of the community that created them.

Eventually everyone passes away, which is to go beyond the seventh sphere and back into the realm of God. Hopefully the solid foundation of your life will ensure an enduring legacy as a monument to your endeavours of life. Such are the gifts of the sphere of Saturn.

Here are some typical phrases from someone undergoing the Sphere of Law governed by Saturn. Do any of them resonate with your own experience? Do you ever find yourself or your friends and family saying them? If so, it is the Saturn within you speaking...

- "I make the rules here."
- "Respect your elders."
- "From my experience, I think you need to..."
- "Hold back and properly consider..."
- "Keep to the law."
- "It's close to the end."
- "I am burdened."

Life is limited, and Saturn is the grim reaper who cuts down the harvest of our years. Whatever is *born* of time, *dies* in time. Saturn brings solidity to structures; it is a tough taskmaster but provides a protective wall, and its restrictions ensure growth and survival as well as death. Knowing that there is a limit to time and life will encourage you to put effort into ensuring all things are done that are needed for a fulfilled life.

This is about abiding by the law—cooperation is necessary so that you fit into the structure that already exists. Your sense of form and structure defines the weight of material responsibilities, which for some can be burdensome. Saturn represents, therefore, the contracting and crystallising tendencies of the ageing process; your form grows hard, rigid, and brittle, eventually becoming ashes and dust.

The journey through the seven spheres may be gentle at first, but as time presses on, you often encounter pain, friction, and resistance as Saturn works relentlessly to purify anything not needed in life. If you follow the rules, you will be satisfied with the end. Otherwise, Saturn, closely connected to the principle of karma, can create a cold stone and a gloomy shadow.

The seven ages

We have seen how the seven spheres, each relating to the essence of a planet, can influence us, both forming as a whole the seven stages of life and, fractally, the contents of each stage. Everything in life follows this order, making it divine—the universal way of the mind. Now we have covered the theory, let's make practical use of it.

5: The New (Old) Perception

Mars—Taking action to refocus

♂

The previous chapters have introduced the seven planets along with their correspondences and ordering. This is the theoretical side of the book, and if you have followed it so far, you are doing well! However to gain the full practical benefit of what we've come to understand from revealing the ancient wisdom of the planets, namely that each inhabits one of seven concentric and humanocentric spheres of influence, we must refocus to shift our perspective. By putting yourself into the driving seat to become the first person again, you can restore your place in the universe.

Shift your perspective

How you perceive reality comes from within you: "All is Mind." Life's experience is that which happens around you. We relate to these things as if standing outside the experience, when, in fact, we are at its very centre. For the last 350 years, we have been taught we are independent observers of all that is, looking at life objectively—the aforementioned *heliocentric* viewpoint. Shifting to a *humanocentric* perspective will shed light on ourselves and how to treat other humans. If you bring everything back into your centre and look out at the world as it revolves around you, a completely different experience will unfold, one that brings personal self-empowerment.

All humans are unified through a collective consciousness; we are aware of living on the surface of a planet orbiting the Sun, along with other planets, which generates a feeling of belonging in the macrocosm. But when you turn the lens around, from the macro to the micro, instead focussing on personal consciousness, you discover a sense of belonging in your own space, one in which your identity is forged and grows.

Knowledge of *the Divine Order* can help you rediscover your own centre and shift your relationship with the Earth and your internal spirit, returning magic to life—the magic of the imagination. Your imagination is infinite and eternal, and there is no limit to how far it can take you.

We now introduce some experiments that will help you connect to *The Divine Order* in creation by unifying your inner and outer worlds and subtly shifting your perspective towards a humanocentric form. These experiments appear very simple, but they may help you understand and discover your true and full imagination and creativity through using your body, your physical presence, along with mindfulness.

Experiment 1: A Jump and a Push!

Making the Earth move

We know that the Earth spins on its axis, traversing a full 360 degrees in a day. Think how large the Earth is and imagine just how fast it is travelling—the answer is an astonishing 1,000 miles per hour. And with our feet planted firmly on the ground, we are travelling along with it at the same speed, yet we feel no motion or giddiness! We are also told that the Earth is orbiting the Sun at a much faster rate, that of 67,000 miles per hour! And again, we are only faintly aware of this by signs such as the changing of the seasons or the gradually shifting patterns of constellations in the night sky.

For the first experiment to recentre your perspective towards a humanocentric form, you need to find a little space to stand up in. Take to your feet and relax. Very slowly, take a short jump or hop into the air. You will find you come back to *exactly* the same spot as before. The movement of the planet has no effect even though for a split second, you were no longer in contact with the planet's surface.

Now, this is easily explained by science, because you yourself were travelling at the same speed before you took off and your momentum keeps you going at the same speed—at least for a short while and if you don't jump too high!

However, if you now change your focus and imagine yourself at the very centre of the whole cosmos, you can change your *perception*. You did not move because you could consider yourself at the centre. Indeed, much of modern cosmology regards the universe as infinitely large, which means that anywhere and everywhere have equal rights to regard themselves at the centre.

So now, imagine the cosmos stretching out in every direction from you, stretching out to infinity, with you at the centre—the humanocentre—of everything, and take another little jump. But this time, it is not you moving, but instead your feet are pressing against the Earth and making *it* move. The pressure from your feet is enough to make the whole planet move downwards, just for a second, before it springs back towards you again.

For anyone keen on keeping fit, you can achieve the same result with a press-up. Lie down on the floor, and press your hands downwards. With your old "third person" viewpoint, the heavy planet Earth stays where it is and your body (hopefully!) moves upwards. But with the new perspective, imagine the equally valid viewpoint that it is your arms that are pushing the planet downwards, away from you.

This simple experiment is the starting point to returning to a more "first person" viewpoint, where you as an individual can regain a sense of identity and a central place in the cosmos. This experiment is a simple one-directional movement, but the next one extends this to a rotational movement, taking us closer to the seven planetary spheres of influence in *the Divine Order.*

Experiment 2: The Unmoved Mover

Being centred in a turning world

You often hear people say that "the world keeps on turning." It is an interesting phrase, and in *the Divine Order,* we recognise two types of motion—primary and secondary.

Primary motion comes from the fact that we stand with our feet on the ground, solid and firm as part of the Earth, and experience the sky rising and space turning above our heads. In fact, the rest of the universe rises in the east (that's sunrise every morning), goes over the top of us during the day, then sets in the west in the evening (sunset). We call that the *primary motion*. You could stand or sit in the same place all day, without walking anywhere, and experience the heavens rising and rotating around you.

But why have we not aligned ourselves to nature—why are we off-kilter with the whole experience? This next experiment is to show you how to place your awareness at your centre of being. To find your own centre point means you can place your mind at rest at its centre. This is very blissful.

Stand up again, and, with a bit of space in which to turn around, point with your finger at your face. With your eyes open, now start turning around on the spot, a full 360 degrees, and again and again. (There is no hurry, so if you feel giddy, just slow down and relax or stop.) If you focus solely on your pointing finger, then is your consciousness moving around, or is it centred, with the world in fact moving around you? It is even a bit blurry!

This movement highlights your point of view and helps to emphasise that there is a still and unmoving centre of being within you where your awareness resides: You are still, and the world is turning. Once again, it is relative but a helpful and equally valid perspective.

Now, hopefully, you have located and become aware of the awareness at your centre. It doesn't move; it never has moved. It is called the *unmoved mover* of the world. It is a place of perfect stillness and peace within you, and one that this experiment can help you reconnect with.

Now try walking along. Once again, the space where your awareness lies is still, and the ground flows under you. In fact, all the scenery of wherever you are flows around the edges, through the periphery, your window of the world. You are constantly moving, but what a wonderful and blissful place to find within, when you experience the world gliding through you.

All transport and movement can be seen from this place of stillness, whether going by bicycle, train, or car. Everything out there is in motion, flowing into the stillness which is here at your centre.

This centred awareness is the first-person position. Most of the rest of the world tends to be in a third-person position. In this way you can see how things arise around you. This is the first place from which to observe your seven spheres of consciousness, emanating outwards.

Experiment 3: The All-Seeing Eye

Becoming immersed in a halo of divine light

So, we have gradually started to become aware of a new perspective by adjusting our awareness of where we are positioned on the Earth and in the cosmos. This will help us perceive ourselves at the centre of *The Divine Order* of the seven concentric spheres that influence us every day and everywhere. But what if you could find a way to change your way of looking at the world in an instant? You may have heard that there is an eye in a pyramid on the back of the American dollar bill. It's called *The Eye of Providence* or *God's all-seeing eye*. It is often imagined to be in the clouds or floating in space, watching humanity.

What if you were given a big reveal and suddenly discovered the capacity to *become* that very same eye? It is not a higher power, unreachable or distant or the arcane knowledge of a secret society. It is within you right here and right now. Many original spiritual books and religious texts talk of "seeing" as the pathway into enlightenment. Most people believe this to be a difficult and disciplined process that can take a lifetime to master, but the good news is that it does not take more than a minute, and this following experiment will open your awareness and change your consciousness in a most positive and uplifting way. Let's begin.

How many eyes are you looking out of now? In your own experience, you accept that you look at the world through a pair of eyes, like two windows in the middle of your face?

Make a pair of binoculars with your hands: Bring your thumbs and first fingers together to make two holes, then move both hands together so

the holes are next to each other, forming glasses. Now slowly put them on, this pair of glasses, by bringing your hands up to your face. Level them with your eyes, so you are looking through them.

Consider how you perceive the world through these two apertures.

As you keep your "hand glasses" on, start to separate your thumbs and first fingers until your glasses turn into a diver's snorkel mask, your hands now framing the edges of your face.

Now gradually spread your hands wider and slightly in front of you, but at the sides, holding them apart so you can bring them back either side of your head, where they both vanish. They disappear into space and then emerge when you bring your hands together again.

In peripheral vision, you see your whole field of view, and it fades out all the way around. However, visually, your attention is drawn to the single space. You are looking out through a great big eye or window—an huge, open undivided space with no edges.

Isn't it incredible that you have spent your whole life thinking you see at the world from two eyes, whereas, in fact, you can have the simplicity and courage just to experience life from a great openness here, a single eye.

Remember it is easy to choose the third eye/all-seeing state or to be in the "normal" world, and you can flip from one to the other as often as you like.

This little experiment is to show you that you too can reside in bliss at your very centre of *The Divine Order*. This is the place from which humanocentricity can grow and evolve because it places you right at the centre of this new way of seeing the planets and their influences on our daily activities and feelings. Do this in nature to make a wonderful new connection to the world where you are at the centre, with the dynamics of the seven planets flowing around the edges of your world view.

6: Release Your Creative Genius

Jupiter—Growing and becoming creative

♃

You have a genius within you—a *genie*—you are ingenious! The seven spheres are the seven big stories of your life. Each one is a chapter in your life, because each reflects a dynamic part of your personality. In this section, we will learn to unlock these genies to release your creative genius and put you in tune with the cosmos. You will write some letters, do some guided visualisations, and practice some breathing exercises.

Meet and get to know your genie

This is a step-by-step process to follow over seven consecutive days. Choose a time when you can devote yourself to this—a weeklong holiday or retreat would be perfect, but in fact, you can do this at any time successfully.

Starting on a Monday, the day of the moon, you will be taken through each sphere of life and working with it on its named day. To get to the essence of each sphere, and bring it to your conscious mind so you can gain insight, healing, and a changed perspective, there is a step-by-step healing process to follow.

There are many astrological systems and techniques that explain the stages of life so it is best to remember that the spheres have a flexible flux, and it is *The Divine Order* that is important; one sphere moves onto the next as a process of evolution in an individual's life. So, although as we have seen, the stages of life follow certain rough ages, it is vital to note that these do not follow the actual order of the modern days of the week. The reasons for this are complex and relate to the planetary hours. Here are the days of the week in order, along with their related planetary spheres and ages:

- Monday (The moon): from birth to age 4
- Tuesday (Mars): age 41–56
- Wednesday (Mercury): age 5–14
- Thursday (Jupiter): age 56–68
- Friday (Venus): age 14–21
- Saturday (Saturn): age 68–98
- The Sun: age 21–41

Your seven big stories will most likely be found within these time frames.

Write yourself a letter

When we were children, before visiting someone, we might write a letter of introduction. Of course, these days, it may be via email or text, but the principle is the same. So, to meet your genie and get to know them well, the best way is by writing to them! In this exercise, you communicate to your sphere, genie, governor, angel, or intelligence by putting your thoughts to them down on paper, in longhand.

Similar to the Aladdin story, the lamp is at first dusty and tarnished. Aladdin decides to clean it; he uses his hands. As he polishes it, the genie is released, and very grateful it is too. The genie (the personal genius, the ingenious) grants Aladdin three wishes as a reward.

Now it is time to get familiar with your own spirit inside of each of your spheres and claim your own rewards. If you are unsure about the spheres, take a quick look at the earlier descriptions of them above to refresh your memory and clarify your understanding.

On each day of the week, take a favourite pen or pencil and write to that day's genie. For example, on Monday, write to the Moon sphere, focussing perhaps on feelings. Write a charming and friendly letter in which you describe the most significant memories of the relevant years of the sphere of the day. It is the active use of your hands writing that will engage your mind and awaken the spirits in the spheres. You can make the letter as long as you like, or, if there are several stories to retell and recount, you might like to repeat the process every week.

Whatever you decide to do, each time you get to the end of writing any letter to yourself, always include this important statement of intent, an affirmation you must remember to write:

> *Thank you (your name), for helping me to remember this part of my life. I love you with all parts of me, and I will always love you.*

Take a little while to contemplate what you are saying to yourself. Then sign and date your letter.

It will be like scanning a searchlight into the dustiest and darkest corners of the attics of your mind. By remembering things long forgotten, re-visualising them, and writing them down, you are cleansing yourself and creating a new space for your genie to express itself. New ideas, new realisations, and a whole new understanding of yourself will arise.

As you clear out your consciousness, so you get to meet your genius—the voice inside your head that governs each sphere in turn.

Once you've been through writing to it a few times, you're going to have a fresh perspective on that planet; that's when you can start to change your life, because you are aware of how that part of celestial intelligence works for you.

You have seven visible lamps, seven planets, each one with a different quality of light you can use. When you enter your cave of treasures (your pure awareness at the centre, the capacity that holds all the treasures of the world) then you'll become aware of your lamps and how you can use them.

When you imagine yourself travelling up and entering a sphere, such that you know what that sphere dynamically represents in your life, then these are questions to ask yourself and write down the answers to.

Why write to yourself? Because the mind stream is very full, and only rarely can one slow it down enough to pluck out specific things. So if you write down what is coming through to you via each sphere, you can actually look at it. And when you see it in front of you, you can do something about it.

Below are some general questions that will help you frame your seven letters. And further on, there are some more specific hints for each of the seven letters.

General points to consider when writing letters to the genies

- What did you yearn for when growing up?
- What do you want now (in context to the sphere you are in)?
- Who were the central figures in your life at that time? Pick out the most beloved, the most encouraging and positive, and then pick out the most negative one, the most repressive to your nature.
- If you could talk to them now, what would you say?
- Recount some favourite memories and also some negative ones.

☽ A letter to the Moon (Monday)

Write about your feelings, the past, mother, & family

The unconscious mind: Do you remember any specific dreams you had when small? How was your imagination? Did you have make-believe characters? Were you an early visionary, seeing things clearly before they happened? Did you talk to your mother about things like that?

Sensory responses: Were you tactile, liking things for the way they felt? Did you have a favourite blanket, food, smell, taste? Did you need a teddy or soft toys? Do you remember your highchair at mealtimes, the comfort of bedtime, or other situations?

Instinctive reactions: When you think about it, do you have any instinctual habits you repeat without thinking? How do you react to and receive the environment around you? For example, do you perceive a change in your feeling or state when you enter or leave a room? Do you absorb everything around you, or does it bounce off you?

Mother: How comfortable did she make you feel? Can you remember her embrace, style of cuddle, how she would enclose you? Do you remember anything of your actual birth?

Nurturing: What are your eating patterns? Do you share food or have a particular style of feeding yourself? How much/how little do you fill yourself? Do you succour others when they need it? Are you a caring sort?

Security and protection: Do you feel strongly about a sense of belonging? Or of safety? Is it important to feel being inside something, to be dwelling within (like being tucked up in bed or under the duvet)? Do you rely on the family or a tribe? Do you enjoy being wrapped up (as if swaddled) in winter layers of clothes. Do you like the idea of entering a cocoon, egg, nest, or a cot, cradle, or just good old comfy bed?

☿ A letter to Mercury (Wednesday)

Write about your school years, ages 7–14

Thinking: Have a think about your own internal dialogue; could you describe your own narrative creation? How do you connect things together? What is your common sense, to you?

Reason & Logic: If you had to explain cause, what would you say? Do you often make judgements in interactions? Are you a deductive and observing type? How do you pay attention when interacting with others? Do you like to define, describe, or justify getting to answers?

Understanding: What are you like with words and numbers? How are your interpretation and translation skills? Would you say you are a knowing person? Are you a storyteller?

Communication: Do you have a style of speaking? What is your writing and handwriting like? Are you an analyst before deciding? Do you sing, play a musical instrument, read musical notation?

Movement: What is your favoured method of getting around: walking, running, driving, cycling? Are you a commuter—do you like to travel? How do you feel about the concept of exchange or trade?

Recognising: Would you say your mental cognition and perception are sharp? Do you discern between things; are you likely to question?

Differentiating: How are you with contrast and difference? Do you easily distinguish between right and wrong, left and right, up and down?

♀ A letter to Venus (Friday)

Write about love and relationships

Relationships: Is there a certain type of person you fall in love with, or do you get emotions for all? In attraction, what situations draw you in? Do you have fancies? When you are coupled or paired up with someone, do your reactions and outlook shift or change? Are you married? Do you believe in marriage? Have you had more than one marriage? Is there a pattern you can discern as to how you are in a marriage? When you admire another, do you do it from afar, or do you make your feelings known?

Value: Is your self-esteem in a good condition? How do you judge your self-worth? Do you thrive with material possessions, or do they weigh heavily? Do you have purchasing patterns, collecting things for example? Are you a compulsive buyer or considered and careful? How do you spend your resources—extravagantly or less so?

Harmony: What sort of music do you enjoy, or listen to? Do you have favourite artists who have influenced your taste and style? Do you feel that life has its own meter and rhyme like a poem? How much cultural interactions do you get involved in?

Pleasures: Is it lovemaking or sex? Do you seek out sensual union? Do you have specific food and drinks that you enjoy? What sort of pastimes do you enjoy that indulge the senses? How do you set about generating contact or touch with others? What sort of things turn you on or off?

Enjoyments: Are you a dedicated follower of fashion? Do you create your own style? Are you a creative dresser with a penchant for dressing up? Are you a socialite who loves to mingle and interact with social groups, friends, or family?

☉ A letter to the Sun (Sunday)

Write about your personal identity and purpose

The I AM: Do you strive for a conscious recognition of the self? Can you say that you are the central focus of your life? Do you recognise the light that shines from within? Is your self-realisation a specific goal in life?

Willpower: How strong is your impetus to get going? Do you feel your dynamic force moving you forwards? Do you want to be something, or someone? Do you perceive how you shine, and is it a conscious force that you identify with? Have you experienced your light being dampened by others? Have you bounced back and restored yourself?

Father: Was your father a good role model? Did he help you to discover your own journey? Did he encourage and motivate you, and show you how capable you are? Would you say that he helped your personality development? Or quite the opposite?

The Heart: Do you experience an inner flame as your spiritual core? How would you describe your radiance and warmth towards others? At your inner centre do you feel compassion and empathy for all? Has this ever been compromised? Would you say that you are growing into love? Have you specifically recognised your life purpose? Does this give you strength from within?

Creativity: How much do you like to show others? Are you a natural performer, or more sensitive, or shy? Do you feel the time to play? Are you on the search for wholeness? Do you identify with a type of creative expression? Is your self-expression outgoing so you can be noticed for what you do?

♂ A letter to Mars (Tuesday)

Write about how you go about setting goals and targets

Motivation: When you get urges, do you push ahead, or hold back? How would you describe your passion? Are you competitive? Do you set out to win? How daring are you? Do you take risks? Are you motivated by sex or sexual desires? How does someone else being sexy motivate you? When you experience anger, does it push you forwards to do something?

Actions: Do you drive? Do you physically exercise? Strenuously, or strategically? Are you assertive or pushy? Are you someone who willingly fights for a cause or provokes to get results?

Leadership: Who goes first—you or another? Are you a starter-upper? Do you have strength you demonstrate, so you can impress? Are you a conqueror? Do you come across as bossy or domineering over others? Are you bold and lead the way?

Direction: Do you consistently move forwards, as if going for a target or a goal? Are you someone who revels in doing or getting on with things? Is life straightforward? Are you spontaneous? If a situation is separating into two, do you stride ahead on your own (new) path, or do you lose focus?

Energy: Are you impulsive? Do you rebound? Are you resilient? What sort of level is your inner and outer strength? Are they comparable? Are you courageous? Do you get easily fired up or hot? How is your energy expressed—do you feel aggressive? Or more passive?

♃ A letter to Jupiter (Thursday)

Write about your faith and beliefs

Faith: Do you have beliefs? A religion? Would you say you are holy? Are you a visionary? Would you take a pilgrimage to seek or quest for a union with your god or goddess? Do you oversee your life and your purpose, taking a big view? Are you righteous? Do you believe in justice? Is wisdom something to develop in life? What are your ethics, and morals?

Meaning: What is your style of learning? Do you have a philosophy that helps you with understanding life? Are you a teacher? Do you feel that "you know?" Are you enthused by something specific? Are you a preacher to others?

Growth: What brings expansion into your life? Do you take opportunities when they come to you? Are you an exaggerator? Do you have the freedom to move or travel whenever you feel to? What is your horizon; is there more to discover or explore?

Benevolence: Would you say you are lucky? Do you attract good fortune? Is your life full of providence? Do you experience abundance? Is there more room for growth? Do you feel protected?

♄ A letter to Saturn (Saturday)

Write about career aspirations, work, and social integration into society

Responsibility: Are you consistently obligated? Do you feel dutiful? Are you disciplined and self-controlled? How serious are you? Are you dependable, consistent, and reliable?

Limitation: Do you feel restricted by circumstance? Are your boundaries well defined? Do you like fences and/or walls? How defensive do you feel about your situation? Is a sense of contraction better than expansion? Do you easily get frustrated? What is your greatest fear?

Ambition: Are you building a career, climbing a ladder? Do you work hard at tasks? How are you when tested? Is life a series of lessons that require achievement? Are you concerned with status and how you are regarded by others? Do you respect your elders? Do you maintain personal authority and self-mastery? Are you embittered if you don't achieve?

Form: How you perceive your reality? Do you enjoy structure? How do you work with time, are you keeping to it? Do you feel to consolidate to make progress? Do things crystallise in your consciousness over time? Is life full of *gravitas*, does it weigh on your shoulders? What is your state of physicality?

Law: Do you follow the rules and orders as set by society, or others? Do you find authority brings clarity? Can you be easily restrained? Do you enjoy slowness and appreciation of time? Do you believe in austerity? Are you seeking solitude or wanting to be a hermit?

Guided journeys within *TDO*

To follow the seven letters, we now present seven guided journeys, one for each planet / day of the week, and an eighth to do anytime to find peace. Each is a kind of story containing the essence of each planet.

Prepare your journey

There are many ways to do this. You could read it first and then revisualise it yourself, ask a friend or loved one to read it to you, or use the versions on this book's website: thedivineorder.co.uk. Once this is arranged, you are ready to take the journey!

Prepare your space

Now, find a quiet and calm space to relax, either lying down or sitting comfortably. Each journey encourages you to connect to your breath as a flowing life force that creates consciousness and acts as a bridge between pure awareness at the centre moving outwards into your wider consciousness.

Set out on your journey

Start breathing in through your nose and out through your mouth, in a cyclic motion. You can, of course, exhale through the nose as well if you wish—whatever is most comfortable. You are experiencing *pneuma*!

Having familiarised yourself with a calm and relaxed breathing motion, begin to connect your breaths together, the inhale and exhale unified into one motion. This is the flowing path, and, as your chest and diaphragm rise and fall, activate the spheres you have become aware of via the experiments in Part 5, lying between your consciousness and the awareness of the emptiness of the void. It is like hatching from an egg, being at a threshold, standing at a frameless window. Enjoy feeling and sensing this edge of creative manifestation, out from which the world appears!

☽ The Moon (Monday): The guided journey of feelings

In which you'll discover your inner light

Starting from your centre, imagine seeing the seven spheres concentrically gathered, translucent in space around you. Visualise yourself moving forward to enter the first sphere of the Moon, a delicate and silvery orb with a super-sensitivity about it. You pick up on instinctual feelings; you feel safe, nurtured, and protected as you perceive its curvature. There is a subtle diffused gloom all around–you can see by it, but it isn't fully clear.

The sphere turns into a bay with a beach, an arc of sand with lightly lapping waves and tides across the expanse. To enter, you must walk between a large pair of carved bull's horns–a gateway, a passage. On one side are white chalk cliffs, glowing in the moonlight, as there is a moon above the water; on the other side lies a calm sea that stretches to a distant horizon.

You have no idea how deep this sea is; you can only see its surface but sense much depth. Gradually an area of water begins to swirl gently in a circular motion, and sea horses appear in these frothy waves, their hooves webbed, their manes seaweed. As the waves part, a lunar maiden appears to rise out of the water. Luna emanates an aura of silvery rays, edged with an amber orb that lightly sparkles with starry light.

She is dressed in a graceful robe with a veil and carries an ornamental lamp, like a full moon, as a guiding torch for the night. This she uses to point up the beach, its diffused light steering her way. As she leaves the water, you see she is not walking but sitting comfortably cross legged on a large crab. You begin to walk beside her; the crab sidles across the beach, and behind it follow thousands of smaller crabs, all scuttling with pincers lifted high, like a connected family or tribe, moving in a set pattern. You smell the salt in the air and seaweed as you wander with this lunar goddess and her entourage. At the base of the cliff, a cave mouth appears, looming out of the darkness. Luna gestures with the lamp for you to enter. As you acknowledge her guidance, she hands you the lamp to hold.

The cave passage slopes down into the earth, where it is moist and damp, cool and dark. Being in this cave makes you feel as if you are returning to the source, the origin, the womb of all life. In this dark underworld, your senses bring forth much imagery of your past and your roots, your lineage and your heritage, your origins and the ones who birthed you, kept you safe and protected, as you grew.

The passage opens out into a chamber where you sit quietly contemplating the rising and falling of your own reactions and responses along with the silent and wordless lunar imagery arising out of the cave darkness.

When you are ready, walk back up the sandy path out of the cave; you hear the sea and reach the beach once more. Luna and her family of crabs have returned to the sea and vanished, the tide has risen and fallen, not even the sand is disturbed.

Now, in the starry and twinkly night sky above the vast ocean, you see a moving display of the lunar phases, like a gentle animation across the horizon–eight shimmering cold light phases. Waxing crescent, to first quarter, full to waning quarter, vanishing to no moon, and then another arc movement of another set of phases.

Within you, you realise that life is all about change; things never stay the same, feelings are like the tides. Adaptation and flux is the everyday response needed.

☿ Mercury (Wednesday): The guided journey of logic

In which you'll enjoy language and ideas

Starting from your centre, move through your spheres to the second sphere of Mercury. You are dressed as a teacher, a scribe, or a messenger, in a long robe.

You have a quill pen in one hand and a scroll in the other. Over your shoulder is a satchel As the sphere wraps round far into the distance, you sense the need to take your message to that place. There is a hint of frankincense in the air mixed with the sweet smell of cinnamon. All five senses seem brighter and more fluent, and your hands and fingers seem lighter, ready to play.

You find yourself standing at a lectern with various people in front of you; some want to do business, trade, or exchange with you. Others are asking to learn from you–they want your knowledge, sensing your ability to teach.

You may feel somewhat nervous, but at the same time, you are curious to explore how you can interact with these people. Your mind is full of wondrous ideas and fascinating subjects to discuss, and it is all this you wish to impart.

You start to measure and compare how you can best be of service, using your quill pen to write onto your scroll your best ideas and notions, the things you will transmit to others.

As you write, you draw on your full agility and dexterity, applying your own analysis and opinions for discussion with the people closest to you.

What you write, you speak, and as you speak, you learn; the reading helps you to think, to make decisions, enquire, and know.

Looking ahead into the curving sphere, you reach across to a hat that strangely has a pair of wings attached to each side of it. You put on your hat, the wings animate playfully.

Looking down at your feet, you see a pair of shoes with pointed toes, and on the shoes, another pair of wings. You perceive that with wings atop and at your base, there is a duality to your essence.

You place your scroll of messages and ideas into the satchel, and with a spring in your step, set off on a well-trodden path.

There are many distractions on the route, but you keep moving and eventually reach a bridge. Halfway across, you meet the person the message is intended for–it is another person a lot like you, dressed similarly, with the same voice. This person has something to give you too; it is also a scroll with a message.

You swap and exchange ideas, and as you do so, you also connect your minds and see emails, texts, letters, telegrams, and messages of all shapes and sizes manifesting in the space before you. These are the conduits between you and another you.

Understanding and knowing your achievements and goals–the two sides to each discourse–allows you to meditate on the complete meaning of the message, the logic of its communication, the learning of its action. As you hear, so you speak, so you increase in mind and logic. The answer is in consideration, so the correct decisions can be made.

♀ Venus (Friday): The guided journey of relationships

In which you'll experience harmony

Starting from your centre, move through your spheres to the third sphere of Venus, where you find love, friendship, and happiness.

Looking down, you see you are wearing a fine light gown made of satin and silk. It is pale green, perfect for enjoying being in the garden, where you find yourself. You have many beautiful adornments–necklaces, bracelets of polished copper inlaid with carnelian, lapis lazuli, and emerald. In your hand, you carry a ripe and juicy-looking apple that is tempting to enjoy.

You can smell roses in the air which soothes you. As you begin to stroll amongst the plants and flowers, following the sweetly scented paths, you see a sparkling fountain up ahead. Go to sit beside it.

Around the fountain are statues in graceful dance postures that seem to have a continuous harmony in their shapes. Stay awhile and gaze at their form.

Now investigating the fountain pool, you find scattered across the bottom many valuable coins, their reflections through the water bringing further delight and a sense of ease; they are your resources, possessions that bring material security whenever needed.

Beside the fountain is a round, handheld mirror and a comb. As you look at your reflection, you see the beauty in yourself, like a reflection of the gardens you are in. Within you now is a beautiful image of your personality, the uniqueness you enjoy sharing with others.

As you look around the garden with its neat and tended beds of flowers and shrubs, you sense a deep sensuous appreciation of every flower and every bloom; in the air there are several fragrances to enjoy. Predominant is rose, and nearby is a bush with deep green foliage and many large pink flowers. As you lean in to sniff a flower, it lifts your spirits, making you thankful for all that is delicately beautiful in life.

You follow a curved path away from the fountain and rose garden, and soon come to a large rectangular table fully adorned with food and drinks of all sorts. Your desires are fulfilled with the sumptuous feast before you, and you wander around the table, picking out your favourite tastes and flavours.

You start to hear the most harmonious sounding music floating through the air, so you continue along the path as it curves around. Soon, another clearing appears with a group of musicians, playing beautiful melodies and harmonies. Them are dancers dressed in pinks and greens, moving around you with grace and ease, seductively flirting with their movement, clearly enjoying the charm they are creating.

You appreciate all of this, and at last arrive at a sumptuous daybed in the shape of a shell, adorned with satins and silks; it oozes luxury and comfort, and as you lie upon it, a sense of delight fills you with sympathy and openness. It is then that your perfectly imagined partner appears, to lie with you in this one-to-one situation. The gardens bring you much appreciation of their aesthetic beauty. This is a place where you could live in peace and harmony.

☉ The Sun (Sunday): The guided journey of light

In which you'll shine

Starting from your centre, move through your spheres to the fourth sphere, which is warm and has a golden light that infuses you with radiance.

As the sphere curves around, you perceive it to be like the path of the sun across the sky. Up ahead, there is a mighty chariot of gold that you step into and experience a triumphant sense of being. There are six horses bridled and yoked to the chariot. This is a vehicle of power. You have in your hands six reins, three for each hand. The horses are champing at the bit and begin to pull you along.

You realise that three of the horses on one side represent the planets Mars, Jupiter, and Saturn. The three on the other side represent the Moon, Mercury, and Venus. Altogether these horses are the other six visible planets, each of which rely on the Sun's light for their own reflection. The Sun is the light giver, and you are directing its chariot, like Apollo, in an arc across the sky.

The Sun, as the central sphere, is the pivotal organising principle of all that is. You are now recognising your purpose, the generating power of your self-development in this lifetime–look ahead, be proud of who you are, and notice how you keep moving forwards; there is no sideways movement, slowing down, or reversing.

You now have a broad survey of all the world and become conscious of how you are beaming light from afar and illuminating the sky. You feel good and unwearied; in this chariot, you are the personal authority, and it makes you feel proud and filled with spirit and energy to be alive. Now you are filling the world with the harmony divine. Agile and warm, you are the world's commander, the source of existence, the supreme lover of the stream. You are the great eye of nature, the faithful defender of all that is good and propitious, the bearer of fruit, the source of the morning light, and the generator of the twinkling stars.

Ride glorious, life is celebrated when you realise you are in and of the light, be the lord of the seasons, guide the good, bless the brightness, live the divine life, the cascade, and the glory at the centre of creation.

This is the kingdom you survey, as your fiery steeds draw you close to a golden palace of domes and pillars, set upon a distinctly grand foundation. You identify with this place which fills you with enthusiasm and confidence.

Inside is a throne room with a precious and important seat of power for rulers and leaders. It is right and natural for you to sit in this.

Your heart is your courage; you become the hero of your own story.

♂ Mars (Tuesday): The guided journey of action

In which you'll motivate and succeed

Starting from your centre, move through your spheres to the fifth one, and, as you begin to immerse yourself in it so it surrounds you, you notice a distinct change of temperature–it is warm, even dry like a desert heat. Looking at yourself, you see you are wearing a red running kit. The ground is dusty and a dark red rust colour, the air is palpably warm and makes you feel hot and dry, and you can taste the heat of chilli peppers in your mouth. There are cacti of all shapes and sizes; you can see their spikes and prongs. Scattered on the ground are large flat rocks, underneath which, in nooks and crannies, lurk a scorpion or two.

A running track stretches out in a circular fashion in front of you. The urge to start running in your mind becomes prescient, and the sense of moving forwards to win takes over, so you begin to move in a direct pace, covering the ground with the intention of reaching the finish line, wherever that might be.

Each side of you are other running lanes, and you are aware you are competing against other energies, which you can sense on either side. It is as if your rivals are flanking you, and you must push yourself to get ahead towards the competition of whatever goal or target you have in mind. The chase is on, and, as you look ahead, you can see shimmering heat, like a mirage in the desert. The heat could burn or scald, but you will go through, using your wild spirit to thrust you forward and penetrate beyond the heat.

The rivals have no faces or forms, they are also an energy, but the sense you must *get it* to *do it* and *take it* makes you bold and passionate.

The more you push yourself, the more vigour and dynamism you feel, your drive and assertion as an individual force makes you happy because it's ***now*** you will win the competition, get up and go.

Drawn on the running track ahead, you see a finish line and instinctively want to cross it; as you do so, so your scene changes.

You look down to see a bow and arrow on the ground. Pick it up and aim into the distance, where you see another target, far away. Taking a shot, you become single minded in action, setting up your goal. You have enterprise, you are the pioneer, the self-starter and the one who takes initiative; you are the winner of your own life.

Your continuous motion forwards brings you an iron helmet on your head, a sword of steel in one hand and a shield in the other. Now you are running uphill to follow and find the arrow you shot, feeling defiance and courage, daring to fight for survival, but also for victory. The uphill struggle leads to a flagpole, the arrow is shot into the pole. This pole you intend to make yours, you have a flag to fly, atop your hill, and you will conquer.

You flex your muscles, feel your strength, and have the guts to push through conflict, take what you want, with nothing to stop you.

As you raise your flag in victory, meditate on the achievement of what it is that you desire, the goal you wish to achieve. That is what is depicted on the flag; you raise it up the pole, above your head, and, in the heat and sweat of your efforts, see it fluttering as a symbol that you have won this battle.

♃ Jupiter (Thursday): The guided journey of growth

In which you'll start to see the big picture

Starting from your centre, move through your spheres to the sixth sphere of the great god Jupiter. Looking down, you notice you are wearing purple robes with numerous yellow stars scattered across their surface. You wear rings of sapphires and amethyst on your fingers and feel magnanimous, high minded, and noble. Climbing up a set of marble steps, a friendly horse tethered to an olive tree greets you. Climb into the saddle, hold the reins, and begin to trot through a wide river valley, full of trees and surrounded by mountains.

Large clouds fill the skies, and you occasionally hear rumblings of thunder echoing down the valley. In the distance, gradually appearing, is a vast cathedral surmounted with fantastic spires and domes. You ride up to the entrance, and, once inside, find yourself in a grassy quadrangle or cloister, with pilgrims circulating and praying for you. It is sacred ground.

With pomp and grandeur, but also humour, you have a philosophy to impart, gained from your wisdom, to preach to these pilgrims; they, with good humour and encouragement, listen to your truths as you show them, benevolently, the greater meaning as you understand it.

This community believe in you, put their faith in you, and direct you through the sacred buildings, which turn into a university of learning, until you reach a dockside, a quay, beside a large ocean. There is a large ocean-going ship waiting there, and you climb abroad via the gangplank. Moving up to the stern, you watch as the ship leaves port, its huge sails billowing in the wind.

Your quest is to expand your faith and beliefs and to explore, to have a visionary adventure. As you speed across this huge ocean, many schools of fish dance beside the ship, some glittering under the ocean surface, others "flying" through the air.

As you roam the waters of the world, so you seek your fortune. As luck has it, a warm and moist wind takes you across the seven seas, and an excess of hot air sees you travelling far. You encounter storms and lightning yet, protected by your feeling of abundance, you become greater, more fulfilled, confident, and inspired.

Your luck and good fortune bring you to a land that is yours, where you can govern through your law, your justice, your system, and your politics, with optimism and generosity.

♄ Saturn (Saturday): The guided journey of law

In which you'll mature and gain long-term stability

Starting from your centre, move through your spheres to the outermost one, the domain of the boundary keeper, Saturn, who provides the limits of your consciousness. Taking you as far as you can go in this earthly, physical, bodily realm of being, Saturn represents *self-mastery*.

As you arrive at the sphere's boundary, the crystalline matrix becomes frosted. Snowflakes drift around; each is perfect in form, but they are cold, and the further you venture into the sphere, the darker it gets. The snowflakes drift out of the darkness and swirl around you, creating a shiver.

You don a heavy cloak, a scarf and a hat, as around your feet, snow and ice clusters gather; to move is to trudge. Progress takes time, so you go slowly.

As the darkness clears, you see you are walking up a rampart made of grey and black stone walls. You perceive you are atop a city wall, a boundary surrounding an inner core.

The sphere curves around, as does the path of this old but strong wall. Looking outwards beyond the wall, you sense an infinite light, the incomprehensible vastness of infinity. It has no form, and you can see how its white light contains all the colours of the spectrum and more. This is felt within you, and the wonderful, all-encompassing view reveals a great deific force, like a creator.

While you have no access to it (you cannot go beyond this boundary wall), out there, you feel in awe of a powerful presence. This is the *Empyrean*, the habitation of the one whose love moves all the other spheres. There is something here so pure and beautiful.

In human form, you cannot enter it… but as you look out, you see that at your centre, lying deep within you, the same light also shines. Your life and existence have, at its heart, a part of the "out there," incarnated into you. You are the light of creation; a small part of the infinite.

Turning your attention now to the inside of this wall, you see a perfect city carefully constructed of solid buildings with precise edges and corners. This city is also arranged in rings, radiating out from a centre point. All the buildings have form and purpose aligned to their rings. These rings are *The Divine Order* of the planets, and the well-proportioned buildings with stable foundations are created from the efforts you are making to understand yourself.

As you work on yourself, so you develop commitment, duty to your own development. You are perfecting yourself as an architect might measure out the perfect dimension of a building. The result is a solid and reliable town plan, well situated and providing good results.

At the very centre of the rings making up your town plan is a monumental building. With its columns, it resembles a temple or law court. This is where you abide by your own laws; this building represents your discipline, maturity, and authority. It is in fact, a beautiful building to behold; it took many tasks and lessons to construct and still has a ladder by its side.

This building represents your ultimate life achievement. What its sanctum contains, once your greatest fear and limitation, is now proof that the work you have done on yourself is rewarded.

The seven spheres guided journey (any day)

In which you'll find divinity always arising, cascading in light

At the beginning, then, start by finding your space within the imagination as correlating with the outside world. Between your awareness and your consciousness is a threshold—a doorway or space between. This is the place between *Being* and *Becoming*.

You are aware of arising out of your creative void, the infinite space of the no-thing, the emptiness which is also the everything.

As you stand in your perfect centre, see the spheres as an expanse; see how you stand at the six directions. These six stretch out equally through your imagined projected spheres with you at centre: You can go forwards, backwards, left or right, upwards, or downwards.

In this moment, in this place, you are held in perfect stillness by what you cannot see.

You are held by the Earth and by the sky; your breath moves the air, each breath giving you a pause for every moment, between being and becoming.

See how you are part of this ever-changing space, of the endless cycles of cosmic creation and destruction.

What you cannot see, you feel instead. By remaining at the centre, you can sense peace and comfort. Be part of this place, created by it, enlivened by it.

All your being is interconnected: "From the arising of this, comes the arising of that."

Each moment invites you to be open and aware, as spacious as the sky that passes through you. Recognize the precious nature of each day. You are always living in a single exquisite moment.

You are standing at the perfect centre of six directions. No matter how off-kilter you feel, you are aware of being in a place of perfectly balanced forces.

You are held by the embrace of the spheres which cannot be seen, but which have a shape, the perfect spherical shape, contained within which is the ordered variety of the seven: one is in all, all is in one. Once you perceive yourself to be here, at its centre, then your mind can relax and rest. One can marvel at the wonderful expanse of just being, whilst also gaining a deep satisfaction from rediscovering this harmony.

Guided visualisations

Do these journeys—or visualisations—as often as you can. By repeating them you will make progress towards your goals (finding something lost, curing unhappiness, gaining something valuable). This is about enjoying being in your newfound space—you are now aware and conscious of being *in light.*

You can create whatever you like in these visualisations, and this is the basis for you to begin to use the *law of manifestation or attraction* in your life. Before reading this book, you might not have known about this choice of perception available to everyone. Now you can choose to be in first person, looking out at the world as a sphere of light in which you are the central figure and creator of all that is. Or, you can be in the original third person, the objective stance that most of the world has been living in for 400 years. Of course, the real magic is that you can now flip from one to the other whenever you like.

7: Bringing It Back to Earth

Saturn—Reflecting and consolidating

♄

We started this book looking a personal journey through life—that of the author. It was an honest telling of events, some happy, others uncomfortable and even painful. But it is a true story, and as such, can reveal much. For the author, it contained a moment of crystallisation; a sea-change in paradigms, and this helped inspire a similar change in the way of looking at the cosmos presented in this book.

We saw how the ancients identified seven planets which moved independently in an otherwise fixed firmament, giving them names, identities, and characters, forming a set of seven archetypes. In Part 3, we learned about both the physical attributes of the planetary bodies and also their metaphysical influences on us.

And in Part 4, we introduced *The Divine Order*, showing why it only includes seven planets and how we need to revert to a humanocentric worldview, where the planets become concentric spheres, spatially distant from us, but exerting a strong influence nonetheless.

In Part 5, we learned to refocus our perspective to rediscover our true nature and place in the universe, using experiments that helped define the difference between awareness and consciousness. These practical experiments are described in great detail, and we hope that the reader will perform them over and over again.

Finally, in Part 6, we met the genies that allow us to release our creativity and reach the peak of our individual potential and manifestation via a series of activities including writing letters and going on guided journeys (meditations), each focussed on a different planet within The Divine Order. These also help with practicing breathwork and introduce the ancient knowledge of *pneuma*, the *animus* and life force.

So... it is now time to put it into practice with some wholesome, practical down-to-Earth examples. Let's see how *The Divine Order* is not simply arcane knowledge or an academic curiosity, but that it can inform and enlighten us in everything from the mundane to the fundamental.

We will first look at flow (considering daily activities and processes) using some examples and case-studies to help get you started with your analyses, and then see how the rulerships of the planets make their own suggestions about timings for those all-important actions, at the level of both days and hours.

These examples are just the start, and we encourage the reader to apply an understanding of *The Divine Order* to their daily life with, we hope, very practical real-life benefits!

Managing flow in *The Divine Order*

Some case studies and processes

The first thing to note is that many processes encompass *The Divine Order* naturally, and understanding this can help us analyse how we do things, and sometimes where we might go wrong. We have seen how the seven planets influence us with their rulerships and characters in turn, and applying this to processes is revealing.

We have chosen four real-world activities—forming relationships, starting a business, buying a car, and buying a house—and show planetary interpretations of the steps involved. This sheds light on how best to achieve each of these actions as well as how things can go down the wrong path or get blocked by getting the order wrong.

These are just random examples we have chosen, and the most important thing is to test it out for yourself. Next time you perform an activity, pause to see which stage you might be at; and what has come before and what might follow. And if you are hitting a block, use your knowledge of *The Divine Order* and the planetary influences to identify the cause and find a solution.

Ultimately this progression is about creating an easy path with natural stepping stones that give you a free-flowing course of action. By tying together each step, life itself flows more harmoniously with inbuilt elegance; if you get the Moon step correct, the Mercury step opens up perfectly. If you get Mercury correct, Venus becomes beautifully clear, and so on. These are just simple development steps to become aware of what could, in turn, make your life more harmonious and move forwards in the right direction.

Example One: Forming Relationships

How many times have you had an instant attraction or fallen in love at first sight? And did the habitual flow of memory patterns stop you from moving forwards with the initial expression? Based on what you've already read in this book, you'll know there's a natural flow stemming from *The Divine Order*, expressing love and relationships.

- **Step one (The Moon):** provides you with senses—you visually see or hear someone.
- **Step two (Mercury):** rationalises those sense responses and you formulate some words (like chatting up). As Mercury rules the hands, then first contact can be made; hugging, holding hands.
- **Step three (Venus):** attracts and brings fancy to the development between you and the other. This can lead to the first kiss.
- **Step four (The Sun):** brings about the sense of self that is lit up and radiates as love has been created. A new level of identification occurs, and the ego is boosted. This is a relationship proper, and both partners are glowing.
- **Step five (Mars):** brings more action, desire, sex, and new goals and targets are set.
- **Step six (Jupiter):** brings expansion and growth—let's go on holiday together or learn something together; what are our faiths and beliefs?
- **Step seven (Saturn):** Over time spent together, responsibility grows, leading to "the rings" of Saturn. Possible marriage, which is a law, and requires orderly duty and commitment, to old age…

Example Two: Starting a Business (a Case Study)

What went through the mind of Steve Jobs, as he created Apple? How can *The Divine Order* be applied to it? Let's see:

- **Step one (The Moon):** Jobs experienced a range of feelings when he looked at early computer interfaces; these may have included frustration at their limitations but awe and excitement at the potentials they offered.
- **Step two (Mercury):** Jobs decided to formulate his own plans and communicate his ideas to the world by forming a company.
- **Step three (Venus):** Jobs needed to give his new device a shape and aesthetic form to realise its potential value. (Incidentally, the company name, Apple, happens to be ruled by Venus.)
- **Step four (The Sun):** Jobs created different products, and they started to shine, and gain recognition. The world was identifying with Apple. And to have an apple gave a boost to the ego.
- **Step five (Mars):** Jobs was now in competition with Windows, this was like a race. Who would win?
- **Step six (Jupiter):** proper expansion and growth led to many more products and an infrastructure; the whole world now knew of Apple, and many put their faith in the brand, and strongly believed in it.
- **Step seven (Saturn):** Apple was here to stay. Thoroughly established, fully foundational, and a governing system that carries huge amount of global authority. The responsibility that comes with that is clear.

Example Three: Buying a Car

When people talk about retail therapy, they are focussing largely on their Venus level of value, self-worth. However, to fully appreciate the power of material goods, purchase and exchange, trade and business, let's see how *The Divine Order* can be used; compulsive buying can be a problem for some people but give things a bit more room in your consciousness and better choices can be made.

- **Step one (The Moon):** I feel I need a (new) car; I visualise what I want—the model, colour, size, shape.
- **Step two (Mercury):** I calculate my budget and go shopping, exchanging money for the object.
- **Step three (Venus):** I consider it an object of beauty. I attach new values to myself because of it. I spend more money to make it look good. I wonder if others will be attracted to me because of it! I look good driving around with the windows down. It plays music.
- **Step four (The Sun):** My ego identity and personality development are affected, I am growing in selfhood because of it. It is becoming an extension of my individual self.
- **Step five (Mars):** I can drive it fast and accelerate. I can race it, putting the pedal to the metal. I can overtake, and I am my own boy racer.
- **Step six (Jupiter):** I can take it long distances, like a chariot to carry myself around. I can explore the distant horizon. I can make space around me.
- **Step seven (Saturn):** There are laws to follow. I must obey authority to allow it to run. I must maintain and fix it over time. It will inevitably get old.

Example Four: Buying a House

A lot of people can spend a lot of time dreaming about their perfect house and might even spend too much time on estate agent websites! When you can see the divine order making its natural order, then some more clarity can be achieved, and the perfect house might well become a reality.

- **Step one (The Moon):** a dwelling place is required in which to be.
- **Step two (Mercury):** Many choices to be made, especially the neighbourhood and local travel connections. The agent is contacted, and business is discussed. Trading dwellings, exchange of contracts.
- **Step three (Venus):** The value of the purchase. What does the dwelling look like? It is nice and agreeable? Does it have a garden? What can be done to improve it?
- **Step four (The Sun):** Now I am in this dwelling I can call it my own. It is the place from which I radiate and identify from.
- **Step five (Mars):** Naturally, I defend my castle.
- **Step six (Jupiter):** I can expand, and grow up into the loft space, or add on an extension. This makes the place bigger and roomier. It makes me feel like a king or queen.
- **Step seven (Saturn):** There is the mortgage responsibility. There is upkeep and maintenance over time. The dwelling will get old. I will get old within it.

These examples give an idea as to how *The Divine Order* manifests itself in the typical processes we go through in life. By understanding this natural flow, we can both go with the influences and also diagnose where and when things might go wrong. Once again, this knowledge can help supply the missing part of the jigsaw and give us specific hints about how to solve problems.

Below is a blank template for you to do some self-anaysis. Think of a process you have carried out and make notes. Does it fit the model?

***Your Example:* ....**

- **Step one (The Moon):**
- **Step two (Mercury):**
- **Step three (Venus):**
- **Step four (The Sun):**
- **Step five (Mars):**
- **Step six (Jupiter):**
- **Step seven (Saturn):**

Managing daily activities in TDO

Influences on daily life

We know that each planet has a specific character and influence on our whole world via *The Divine Order*. And of course, each planet is linked to a day of the week—the seven visible planets is probably the reason why there are seven days of the week.

Some of the names of the days in English still reveal their planetary origins, though other influences have been brought to bear, and the English week has ended up with a mixture. It is interesting to compare this with other languages, such as French:

Lundi = "Moon day" (Monday)
Mardi = "Mars day" (Tuesday)
Mercredi = "Mercury day" (Wednesday)
Jeudi = "Jupiter day" (Thursday)
Vendredi = "Venus day" (Friday)

Because of the planetary rulerships (see Part 3), there are specific influences indicated for each day. This implies that certain activities may be highlighted on a specific day and that certain events may also be more likely to occur. Of course, *any* event could take place on *any* day or may not even happen, but it may be helpful to focus on these daily planetary influences, mediate on them, and understand how they influence our life.

As with all aspects of *The Divine Order*, it is the interpretation of the influences which is vital, and this only gets better with practice and understanding. So we are including a handy and concise guide to the week, including observations, correlations, and activities that may be highlighted on a certain day. It might be a good idea to take notes when you make a discovery or when an otherwise unexplained coincidence occurs to see how the patterns start to evolve. This knowledge and understanding can be very helpful in dealing with daily life.

Daily Activities

On each specific day (e.g., Monday, Tuesday, etc.), focus often on the planet that rules it. Where convenient or comfortable, recall the planet in question, creating a clear mental picture so you can integrate it into your life and make it a reality.

It is vital when working with your spheres to see the natural progression they fall into place with: Sensory stimuli turn into feelings, which turn into thoughts, which turn into deeds, which turn into purposes, which turn into actions, which turn into truth, which turn into reality.

The spheres all need each other, so at the same time, consider them—and yourself—as a holistic system. This is empowering because, instead of randomly wanting to make a change in just one isolated area of life, you are now looking at the parts that make up the whole and focusing on their natural and divine order. May this power be yours!

Always remember to feed your spheres with positive energy. What you wish and desire must be ever clearer; picture yourself receiving, achieving, imagining that which you want or need.

Allow yourself change and variation so you can make adjustments and go with the flow. You might have started with a specific intention, but sometimes that will change and shift—let it! Accept that life is impermanence, things change all the time, nothing stays the same.

☽ On the day of the Moon (Monday)

In general, Mondays are perfect for being at home, doing all the regular household chores (laundry, cleaning) and staying as calm and centred as possible. Take note how most of the modern world has not been doing that for a long time. If you observe society as a whole, how would you say people react, feel, and respond on a Monday?

Below are some aspects of life which are related to the Moon and Mondays for you to consider. As you learn about these, look back to the rulerships of the Moon. Can you see how they are connected?

- diet / cooking / eating with friends or family
- contemplating calm / dreaming / meditating
- making plans
- reconciliation and love
- yoga
- reading a book or telling a story.
- artistic expression (painting, poetry, music)

☿ On the day of Mercury (Wednesday)

In general, make Wednesdays the day for important phone calls, emails, or texting. It is perfect for networking. If you've got a lesson to teach or a message to impart, now is a good day to act on it. What is often referred to as hump day—the halfway point in the working week—is also the connecting point that Mercury represents: it fuses together two parts acting as a connector.

- communicating ideas / writing emails / composing letters
- doing business or trading
- sorting out a diary or calendar
- learning / doing a course or evening class
- working with your computer /sorting out your desktop and software
- avoiding a rush / information overload

♀ On the day of Venus (Friday)

In general, this day is for affability and friendliness. It is perfect for going on a date (especially a first date!), making friends, building relationships, and having a good time. Enjoying shopping, spending money on yourself and others, and generally picking up good vibes.

- planning finances
- building and improving relationships, partnerships, and friendships
- developing artistic skills and expression
- spending money on yourself as well as loved ones / pampering yourself
- appreciating cultural pleasures, art galleries, music concerts
- mediation and reconciliation after disagreements
- avoiding confrontation and difficult situations

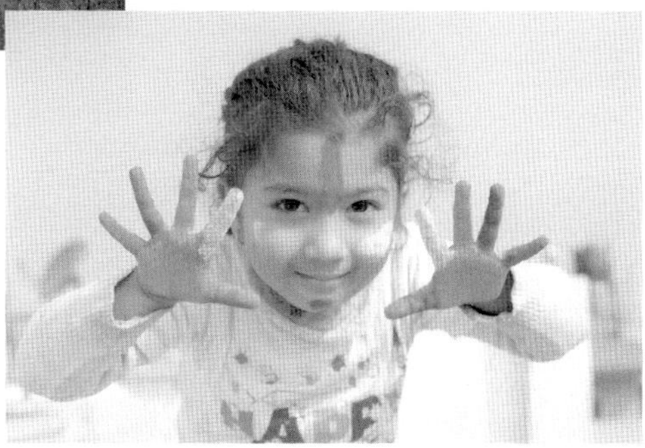

☉ On the day of the Sun (Sunday)

In general, Sundays are for recharging your core sense of self, the battery of life. This is a day in which it is important to do something you enjoy, and you can completely be yourself. A lot of people say be "easy like Sunday morning" and it is a time to be good to yourself. Think of your vitality, self-expression, and purpose on this day.

- shaping your true purpose / developing a sense of self
- being self-expressive / promoting yourself
- improving health
- being a good person / a spiritual awakening
- enjoying fruitful pastimes
- meeting important and influential people
- your increased ability to make decisions
- avoiding indecision, weakness, and boredom

♂ On the day of Mars (Tuesday)

In general, Tuesdays, being ruled by Mars, have a much more energetic influence and are an ideal day for acting or driving forwards with plans already set (on the Monday). Use the motivating energy to set your goals and drive you forwards into the rest of the week. Use outward and outgoing energy to get things done—a day for achievements.

- becoming determined / moving forwards with plans
- being courageous / setting targets
- showing leadership skills / taking the initiative
- physical exercise (gym / running / jogging / cycling)
- the start of something, especially adventurous
- avoiding stress, confrontation, or overexertion

♃ On the day of Jupiter (Thursday)

In general, Jupiter is the day of optimism and bold moves. This is really the day of manifesting what you want in life. Attune to its lucky vibe and expand and grow into it.

- giving help and advice to others
- gaining a deeper understanding of personal philosophy, faith, or belief
- being hopeful and optimistic
- looking after yourself
- starting a venture
- making new friendships
- avoiding excess or overindulgence

♄ On the day of Saturn (Saturday)

In general, this is the Sabbath, the last (or sometimes first) day of the week and the day of rest. Saturn takes things slowly and so must you. Contemplate your achievements and don't put too much pressure on yourself. Saturn can be linked to prohibitive energy, although it can be the busiest day of the social week in many countries.

- keeping to the long-term plan / being disciplined and durable
- appreciating that some things take their time, are slow, or delayed
- becoming more controlled / showing personal authority
- managing daily tasks—housework and gardening
- getting advice from those who are wise
- remaining adaptable
- avoiding or removing blockages

Going beyond...

As you can see from the previous examples, *The Divine Order* is a flowing system showing how to move forwards in life, in both processes and daily activities. If you would like to add a little finesse, however, an extra benefit is to be gained from the knowledge that the *planetary day* is especially effective when used with the same *planetary hour,* which happens four times during each 24-hour period.

Before clocks were invented, the ancient concept of time was that a "day" (named after a planet) started at sunrise and carried on through to the next sunrise of the next day, essentially covering the equivalent of a 24-hour period.

The hours that made up the day were daylight hours followed by nighttime hours. They were often measured using an hourglass orb. Because of the variance of sunrise times throughout the year—sometimes earlier, sometimes later—the measurement of time was referred to as the *unequal hours.* Once mechanical clocks were invented and adopted by society, a more rigid system developed, which, although mechanically precise, lost out on its natural Earth-based connection, leading to an increasing disenchantment. A return to hours based on *The Divine Order* may help!

There is a very simple way to work out the planetary hours if you are interested, and you can find that in Addendum A at the back of this book.

Afterword

The key to happiness

☺

Using the wisdom gained by the knowledge of how the planets influence us, what might have been a life experienced as a chaotic journey can now be managed with specific milestones on an ordered path of personality development through time.

As you overcome any problems experienced (using your seven stories), you will supercharge yourself to recreate and become a divine human being, living in the heart of the creation! This is the key to happiness and appreciation of all that is.

In everyone, there is an artist, writer, composer, musician, singer, poet, seeker, learner, traveller, and healer, among many others. You can create and manifest all these skills to become happier and more content with the infinity of the unfolding universe of which you are an integral part.

This book has shown you how to change your perspective and look out from your centre, and thus see your world and perceive life differently, understanding yourself as an immortal soul of pure infinite awareness. Once you connect with the creation and find that source of infinite awareness at your centre, you will completely transform your creative process.

The goal of *The Divine Order* is to bring together into unity our awareness and consciousness so that we are supremely satisfied with all. This book hopes to bring you beautifully to your humanocentric locum, to discover a new vision of reality which is all the dynamic glory of divine creation. Heaven's realm can be stored and treasured in the mind; one must move into the heavenly arena like a descending ray of light.

Towards a Gaiacentric revolution

As we conclude our journey through *The Divine Order*, it is perhaps appropriate to highlight the urgency with which we need to re-establish the interconnectedness not just with the planetary spheres but with human and planetary life.

If you do the exercises in this book and understand how the world revolves around your pure awareness at centre and the development of ego consciousness, you will also see how it all fits into the oneness and unity of life on planet Earth. This is revolutionary because we absolutely **must** change our direction of consciousness—and quickly—so we can be at one with the living network already here.

Having been through heliocentricity, we have a renewed understanding of our place in the universe, a geocentric and hence humanocentric viewpoint. However, as mentioned earlier in this book, the Earth is not just a piece of rock but a living infrastructure of its own within *The Divine Order*, and one that includes us. So the next stage is to move from a humanocentric viewpoint towards full *Gaiacentricity*. And this will be Book 2 in this series.

Glossary

archetype: *an idea, image, model, symbol, emblem, or original pattern from which myths, stories, and meanings are formulated and develop; images of a collective nature, found naturally arising in the psyche of humanity; a symbolic and universal nature recurring in characters or ideas found in literature and art and all branches of creative expression; often seen as unconscious patterns of behaviour, closely linked to instincts that motivate human behaviour*

awareness: *discernment or vigilance of something happening or existing at the present moment based on information or experience; implies a state of being gained through one's own perceptions or by means of the five sensory inputs; brings about a watchfulness or a condition of being spatially aware of oneself*

centrifugal: *in reference to the superior planets above the Sun, the tendency to move outwards, fly out, proceed outwards from a centre*

centripetal: *in reference to the inferior planets below the Sun, the tendency to move towards the centre*

consciousness: *the state of being awake, thinking, and responding to one's surroundings; the collective thoughts and feelings of an individual; what passes in the mind during the waking state as internal knowledge and understanding and realizing it thoroughly; knowing or perceiving within oneself an inward and awake mind endowed with active mental faculties; a state of being, characterised by sensation, emotion, volition, and thought*

cyclic: *circular or moving in a circle such that it repeats and returns into itself; indicates motion like a turning wheel*

diurnal: *active in the daytime or a behaviour that occurs in the daylight; performed in or occupying one day; of or belonging to one day; repeating once every 24 hours (from the Latin diurnalis "daily, happening every day")*

feminine: *used in astrology as a technical word that helps to differentiate the quality or nature of a planet; similar to "negative," as in a planetary nature inwardly expressed or receptive*

fractal: *a curve or non-regular geometrical shape, found in nature and in the human form, in which similar structures recur at increasingly smaller scales, thus creating what appears to be never ending patterns; natural fractals help explain humanity's universal and innate subconscious understanding of the world; provides a model for natural systems that grow over time, from the microcosm of individual human parts to the macrocosm of the Earth, a comparison bringing intuition, aesthetics, and a spiritual understanding of creation*

gravitas: *seriousness, solemnity, weight, and heaviness*

inferior: *in reference to the order of the seven visible planets, to be low, lower in position, farther down, or below or beneath (the Sun); Inferior planets are those which have their orbit between the Earth and the Sun (The Moon, Mercury and Venus are inferior)*

macrocosm: *the great world, in which there is an order or harmonious arrangement; the whole, or the complete structure, like a universe; a complex or organised system considered a single unit*

masculine: *used in astrology as a technical word that helps to differentiate the quality or nature of a planet; like the use of the word "positive," as in a planetary nature outwardly or upwardly expressed*

metaphorical: *an enlivening form of creative use of language and description, deepening the meaning, in which one group of words is used to stand for, or represent, another group of words usually classified separately from one another, e.g., implicit comparisons made between human emotions and the weather: "He was stormy; She was bright;" "His wit is dry; they are cloudy."*

microcosm: *where the human form represents and encapsulates in miniature the characteristics of the universe and the resulting correspondence between the universe and man; literally understood to be a miniature world*

nocturnal: *active in the night or a behaviour that occurs in the dark*

perception: *the ability to see, hear, or become aware of something through the senses; a form of comprehension or awareness, a mental grasp of objects; organisation and interpretation of sensory information to make sense of the world*

periodic: *a successive series of revolutions; something returning at fixed intervals*

pneuma: *an ancient Greek word meaning the vital force, soul or spirit of a person or living thing; "air in motion" or breath; considered necessary to life; linked to inspiration and influence, words indicating the play of spiritual wind or movement of air, as spirit, or part of life force*

psyche: *the animating principle of the human mind; this animation is in close relation to and directs the human body; it occupies the mind as the seat of thought, feelings, desires, and affections. It provides understanding and the faculty of reason and is the seat of the human soul, an essence that differs from the body and is not dissolved by death. The divine breath of pneuma (q.v.) that is breathed into man, is a higher and purer entity that feeds Psyche.*

superior: *(in reference to the order of the seven visible planets) situated above, higher in position, upper, or over and above (the Sun)*

temperament: *a person's nature determined in four categories, which defines their behaviour, personality traits, and how they might interact with the world; also the four elements, Fire, Earth, Air, and Water, associated with Choleric, Melancholic, Sanguine, and Phlegmatic*

Trivium: *the three ways; a body of knowledge and learning encompassing the three Liberal Arts (grammar, logic, rhetoric); the root of understanding and using language to communicate, apply reason, and persuade; each subject is ruled by an inferior planet: The Moon: grammar, Mercury: logic, Venus: rhetoric; has formed the backbone of classical education for over 2,000 years; at core teaches the student to "know thyself" through refining language, thought, and speech.*

Quadrivium: *the four ways; the four liberal arts associated with numbers (arithmetic, music, geometry, astronomy), which, with Trivium (q.v) comprise the Seven liberal arts; the superior planets rule each subject: The Sun: arithmetic, Mars: music, Jupiter: geometry, Saturn: astronomy; a sacred study of knowledge considered by Greek philosophers at the heart of understanding the soul, and required to ascend to unify back with the source of creation. From a metaphysical perspective it can be said that 'Man is measurement', as the soul evolves and grows firstly through Arithmetic (calculating number); music (number in time); Geometry (number in space) and Astronomy (number in space and time).*

Addendum A: Planetary Hours

As we have seen, the days of the week hold a special significance, and each has its own rulerships, things to consider doing, and things perhaps to avoid on that day.

Monday: The Moon
Tuesday: Mars
Wednesday: Mercury
Thursday: Jupiter
Friday: Venus
Saturday: Saturn
Sunday: The Sun

However, for anyone who wants to gain extra subtlety and understanding, it's helpful to learn more about the planetary days and planetary hours. For example, to get the most powerful result for a Sun meditation, the perfect time do perform it would be on the day of the Sun and during the hour of the Sun.

For the ancients, the day began with the sunrise and ended with sunset. Imagine a world without artificial lighting; especially in winter; the sunlight hours would be all-important for everyday activities. Of course, sunrise and sunset vary greatly around the world and during the year. Some areas in the far north even experience permanent daytime for months followed by permanent night, with huge impacts on daily life!

These ancient days and nights are themselves divided into "hours," each named after the planet which rules that time. As we have learned, there are seven visible planets, and a 24-hour period thus has three complete rotations of these planets (7 x 3 = 21) with three hours left over. Having read this book, you may be guessing that *The Divine Order* is somehow connected, and if so, you would be correct! In fact, the rulerships of the planetary hours follow that of *The Divine Order* exactly, moving in an anti-clockwise direction, i.e.,

Saturn > Jupiter > Mars > The Sun > Venus > Mercury > The Moon

So, we now need to know how to work out exactly when the planetary hours are. This is a very specialised and complex procedure, but we will present a unique and simple way for you to work these out!

When is an hour not an hour?

There is a quandary and paradox when we look more closely. Imagine the sunrise is early, around 5am, and sunset is late, around 9pm, something you might find, say in the UK in summer. This means we have 16 hours of daylight and 8 hours of darkness. However, we still divide the day and night into twelve "planetary hours." This means that each of the daytime planetary hours is longer than 60 minutes. And to compensate, each of the nighttime planetary hours is less than 60 minutes. Thus, they are sometimes called the "unequal hours." To our modern, equal-tempered world, this sounds very odd, but to the ancients, it made complete sense, and it is what we must work with.

How to find the planetary hours

Finding the first hour

If it is, say, a Wednesday—the day of Mercury—we want to find the Mercury hour. Or if it is a Monday, we want to find the Moon hour. The first such hour is easy—it is sunrise time! One way to find this is to sleep with your curtains open so that the first rays of light naturally awaken you, at which point, you know it is the planetary hour of that day! For any heavy sleepers, the second way is even easier, as it's usually printed in the newspaper or shown on most smartphone weather apps.

In fact, on a Wednesday, there will **always** be four Mercury hours, and on a Monday, there will **always** be four Moon hours, and so on. And it is these convergences that are traditionally the most powerful times to perform some action. The first hour of the day is not always the most convenient moment, however, so how can we work out when the other three are?

Finding the other three hours

Because there is such a wide variation of sunrise and sunset times across the world and throughout the year, there are complex tables available that can give exact details. However, our method is simple and straightforward, and will work at any time of year in any location. Let's see how it works, step by step!

Step 1: Draw a circle

You can do it by hand, use a compass, or draw round a cup.

Step 2: Mark out the hours

Divide your circle into 4 equal parts:

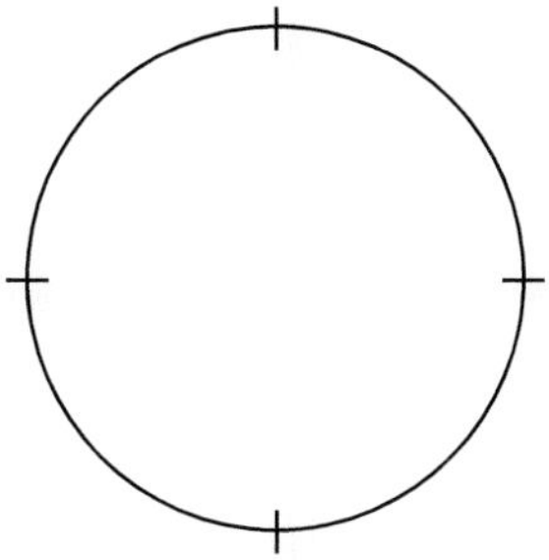

Step 3: Fill in the hours

Make a 24-hour clock face. Divide each of the quarters into six roughly equal parts. Add the times as shown:

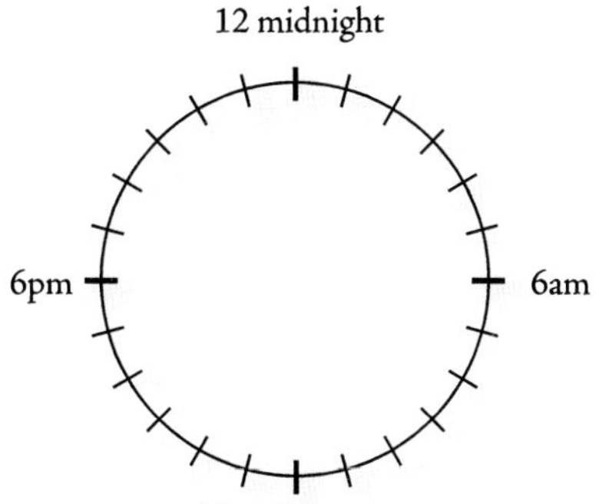

Step 4: Add the sunrise and sunset

Find the times that the sun will rise and set. Mark those on your clock face. Let's use the example above, of 5am and 9pm. Join these to the centre.

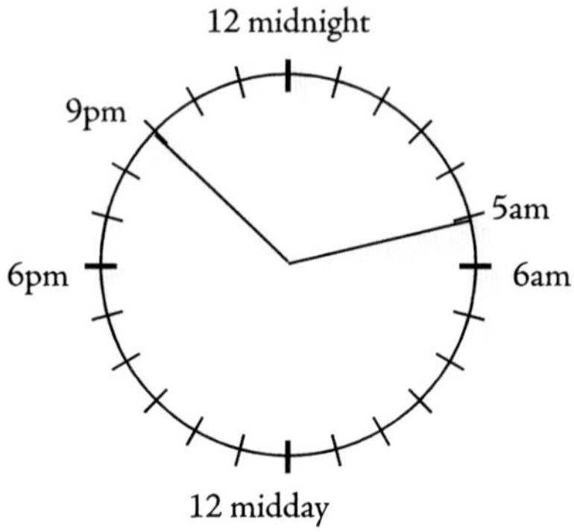

Step 5: Find the mid-points

Look at the two spaces you've created. Try to draw the line that cuts each one in half. This will show you exactly when the planetary hours of that day take place:

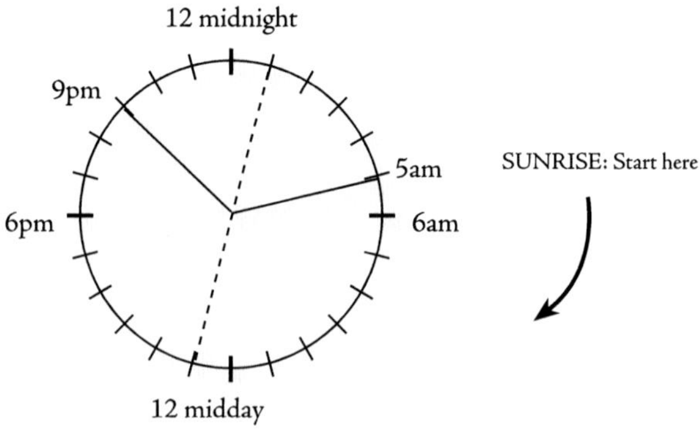

In this case, you can see that the planetary hours of the day begin with sunrise, at 5am. The next one will be at 1pm, followed by the third one at 9pm. There is one more, in fact, which takes place at 1am. Of course, for us, this is actually 1am on the following day if you want to be very strict! The next day will begin at sunrise the following morning.

If the day we are using is, say, a **Saturday**, then the **Saturn** planetary hours will be at 5am, 1pm, 9pm, and 1am (actually on *Sunday* morning according to the calendar). If the day is a **Wednesday**, these hours will represent the **Mercury** hour—good for, say, communication.

Other planetary hours

We mentioned that the planetary hours follow the sequence of *The Divine Order* in reverse, so the Saturn planetary hour will always be followed by the Jupiter planetary hour, and then Mars, etc. Depending on your location and the time of year, and also whether it is day or night, the planetary hour might be more or less than 60 minutes. This makes it very complex to calculate and also leads to interesting combinations, for example, the Venus planetary hour on the day of the Moon (Monday). This is beyond the scope of this book, but anyone interested in learning more will find information in the next book in this series or on the book's website at thedivineorder.co.uk.

Addendum B: Inferior vs Superior

Saturn ♄	Superior	... so without As above... Ex•terior Ex•act Ex•tend	Freeze	The impersonal world	Public life
Jupiter ♃			Flight		
Mars ♂			Fight		
The Sun ☉	Balanced and measured In-between Radiance of self				
Venus ♀	Inferior	As within... ... so below In•terior In•side In•timate In•nate In•stinct	Emotions	The personal world	Private life
Mercury ☿			Words		
The Moon ☽			Feelings		
The Earth	The corporeal body The five senses The centre of being, pure awareness looking out at the world				

The flow of the inferior and superior planets

We experience life under the light of the great central Sun, the fourth of the seven-planet *Divine Order* array. This grouping can be divided into *superior* and *inferior* planets, though these terms do not refer to their everyday usage of "better" or "worse," but instead simply come from the Latin words for "above" and "below" respectively. Let us see why this is.

Each side of the Sun lie three planets: The first three are inferior as they orbit in-between us (on the Earth) and the Sun. Thus, if we are standing on the Earth, looking up into the interlocking and nested, rotating, crystalline spheres above us, we find the Moon first, then Mercury, then Venus, and then the Sun.

On the other side of the Sun are the three superior planets: Mars, Jupiter, and Saturn. These orbit around us further away from the Sun and take longer to complete their cycles. Thus, they are considered "outer" or "exterior" planets.

Interestingly, you may have noticed that the days of the week do not follow *The Divine Order*:

The Moon >	Mercury >	Venus >	The Sun >	Mars >	Jupiter >	Saturn
Mon >	Wed >	Fri >	Sun >	Tue >	Thu >	Sat

The reasons for this order historically are complex and will be covered in more detail in future books in this series, but it is clear that the progression alternates between the inner and outer planets, with the great central Sun positioned in the middle, and this allows consciousness to remain in an equidistant space, as the journey of our souls straddles the binary influences of the superior and inferior planets.